What Do I Say to a Friend Who's Gay?

What Do I Say to a Friend Who's Gay?

Emily Parke Chase

Kregel
Publications

What Do I Say to a Friend Who's Gay?

© 2006 by Emily Parke Chase

Published by Kregel Publications, a division of Kregel, Inc., P.O. Box 2607, Grand Rapids, MI 49501.

Library of Congress Cataloging-in-Publication Data
Chase, Emily Parke.
    What do I say to a friend who's gay? / by Emily Parke Chase.
        p.   cm.
    Includes bibliographical references.
    1. Homosexuality—Religious aspects—Christianity.
I. Title.
BR115.H6C43   2006
261.8'35766—dc22   2006026419

ISBN 0-8254-2435-6

Printed in the United States of America

06 07 08 09 10 / 5 4 3 2 1

*For the "mighty men" who uphold me
with their friendship.*

Author's Note

In the book, some names and facts have been changed to protect the privacy of the individuals who have shared their stories. Names that appear in quotation marks (for example, "Barb") have been changed and should not be associated with individuals whom the reader may know personally.

A portion of the profits for this book will go to help support the work of Exodus International, a Christian ex-gay ministry.

Contents

Preface

- What can I say to a friend who is gay?
- Is "gay" contagious like a disease?
- Can I still be friends with someone who's gay?
- If we remain friends, won't people talk?
- How do I know if the relationship is getting too physical?
- If it gets too physical, what should I do?

If one of these questions has crossed your mind, you may be missing out on the joy of helping a friend who is hurting. You may be more concerned with what people might say about you than you are about your friend's feelings. If so, you're not alone. Lots of your peers are asking the same questions and have the same fears. Before you get all bent out of shape, consider this: Maybe it's our world, not you, that's warped. Perhaps the problem doesn't lie with you at all.

There's another question many people are afraid to ask out loud. They look over their shoulders to see who might be listening, and then they whisper, "What if I'm gay?" That question is followed by a flood of other ones:

- Do other people ever wonder if they're gay?
- If I like someone who's the same sex as me, does that mean I'm gay?
- If someone calls me a queer, does that mean I am one?

- For that matter, doesn't my thinking about these questions mean I already know the answer?

Whoa! Slow down! The chapters that follow are full of stories of young people like you—people who've struggled with these questions. Many of the individuals in the book have heard people snicker, "They must be gay."

Here are some other hard questions:

- Where does God fit into this picture?
- Is being gay the unpardonable sin?
- Does God hate gays?

By the end of this book, you'll find some answers and, along the way, discover three important facts: strong same-sex friendships are a gift from God; people facing same-sex attraction need friends as much as anyone else does; and God himself yearns for your companionship. He, above all others, desires to be your best friend.

Here we go on a really unique trip. Hang on for the ride!

Acknowledgments

A book is never a solitary work. This book owes its life to the many people—gay and straight—who've shared intimate details about their personal lives.

Special thanks go to Tom Baker, Heather Masshardt, and others who critiqued the manuscript from their youthful perspective. I also appreciate the encouragement and guidance of Bob Davies, former North America director of Exodus International.

And thanks to my ex-gay husband, Gene, for sharing his expertise of twenty-five years in ministry to men and women struggling with homosexual temptation.

1

Help!
My Friend Is Gay!

What follows is the personal—very personal—story of Tom, a young man who came out to his friends at a Christian college. His heart was broken, his faith shaken, and his trust betrayed when his friends misunderstood his cries for help.

I began my journey "out" in 1995. I went to a local Christian bookstore to buy a copy of *Coming Out of Homosexuality* by Bob Davies and Lori Rentzel.[1] I was *so* frightened that someone might see me or recognize me. When I arrived, I located the book on the shelf. Then I walked around the store to make sure that I didn't know anyone. I picked up the book, read a page or two, quickly put it back on the shelf, and walked around again to make sure it was safe. Each time I returned, I followed the same procedure. I think I must have done this ten times.

After two return trips to the store and repeating the same thing all over again, I mustered all my courage, grabbed the book off the shelf, and approached the cashier. Wouldn't you know it—it was a guy! I was breathing so fast and my heart was pounding in my ears. I laid the book upside down on the desk and engaged him in rapid-fire conversation to take his focus off the title. My hands were sweating and shaking. I almost passed out. I wanted him to be distracted, and to my surprise it seemed to work. He didn't even look uneasy.

Phew! That was my very first small step in coming out.

I took this book to a local park and sat under a beckoning, ancient oak tree. The tree was so strong—it seemed so grounded and stable. I needed that support because, at that time in my life, I was alone with this struggle. I leaned against the tree and peered over the lake. My legs were still shaking, and I had goose bumps. I can still hear the sounds of the birds and the waves in the water, and feel the cool breeze on my skin. What a memory! The strength of the tree trunk at my back comforted me.

I prayed a soft prayer and began reading. Being careful so no one would see me or what I was reading, I read that book from cover to cover. The well-written stories drew me in. With the last page, I noticed in the back of the book a reference for a local ministry offering help to those who had questions regarding homosexuality. I certainly qualified! With tears streaming down my cheeks, I looked out over the lake and decided right then that I'd call.

I went to see the man in charge of the ministry and, off and on, over the next year and a half, we met in his office. I think that the first answers to all my questions and self-doubt came from this man of God. I felt relieved that someone besides myself now knew, and I didn't have to carry my load alone anymore. With his encouragement, I even decided to attend college again. My studies began in the fall of 1997. This decision would impact my life in a way I could never have imagined.

I can describe my experience at the college as bittersweet. Sweet because I was popular, well liked, involved in the student body, making many new friends, and having a good time.

I have to say it was also bitter because of the circumstances I'm about to share with you now. The memories flood my mind even as I write these words. I met a person I'll call "Adam." Over the course of time, our friendship deepened. He had a girlfriend, "Jessica," and we three became good friends. We hung out a lot, shared a lot, and enjoyed each other's company.

Jessica was the first fellow student who I came out to. She took it well. In fact, she and I talked at length one night about what my life had looked like up to this point. She asked me some very intelligent questions and cared about my responses. I could feel it. It felt so good to know that someone else knew about me and still loved and cared for me.

Again, it was affirming to me that I no longer had to carry this burden alone. I could count on the help of others. Sure, those in ministry had expressed their appreciation and care for me, and I needed that. But this was the first peer who I came out to, the first real friend who didn't "owe" me any type of ministry. Her affirmation meant a lot to me. My friendship with her deepened, and she became a trusted confidante. Over time, we hung out more and more.

Adam could sense that Jessica and I had a special friendship and was actually growing a little jealous. Sensing this, Jessica encouraged me to talk to Adam about my life issue, but I was scared to death that he would react like a typical male and end a friendship I counted on and valued so highly. I looked up to him more than he realized. She kept at me because she felt Adam was being excluded. At last I agreed that he should know. I asked to speak to him alone one night.

When we met, we talked about everything *but* homosexuality. I knew he already suspected what I wanted to tell him about myself, but that didn't allay my fears. I was petrified. He was confused and a little disappointed when I didn't tell him because he knew that I had something on my mind. It was too much for me that night, however, so I left without telling him. I drove around for a while and then just stopped the car at a pay phone, dialed him up in his room, and blurted out, "I used to be gay." Then I hung up. It's actually kind of funny and tender at the same time, now that I think about it.

When I returned to my room I locked the door and called Jessica to tell her. She was happy, and she told me that Adam had already called her. She relayed a message from him: "Tell Tom I love him." I

knew it was going to be okay from then on. Adam even came to my
room and knocked that evening, but since the door was locked, he
knew I wanted to be left alone for the moment. Later, after returning from some personal business, I found a note, which Adam had
written and left on my desk.

It said, "(1) I love you. It's unconditional. (2) I expect a *big* hug
from you in the morning."

I still keep this note in a special place to this day. I must have
read that note a hundred times since then.

The next morning, and many times thereafter, I received that
hug. I was so thankful that he knew about me and yet was still
okay with hugging me. Most guys I know wouldn't have done that.
I remember how much I cried that night as the feelings of acceptance and love overwhelmed me, probably for the first time in my
life. I can't describe how these two individuals made me feel. Oh
how I loved them both for it. They were my Jesus with skin on. So
powerful! I had longed for an expression of him for so very long
within the body of Christ. They modeled to me, both personally
and relationally, what I had previously only heard about in books,
in sermons, in prayers, and from other people.

Up to this point, I strongly believed that this kind of love was not
available to me or to people like me, and it never would be. I began
to trust once again. Perhaps I was wrong about my grudge toward
God and the church. Perhaps I could learn to love and allow myself
to be loved once again. I felt hopeful. Maybe God was trying to tell
me something.

Following my disclosure, everything went well. From time to
time, as their curiosity and desire to be educated grew, Adam and
Jessica asked me questions. They even helped me through the process of coming out to my family. All the while, each of them reaffirmed that their love for me was unconditional and that no matter
what I told them about me, it was okay. I felt safe. Our friendship
deepened.

Before summer vacation, Adam gave a stuffed animal to me for
a keepsake since we'd be missing each other and couldn't see each

other as often as we might like. I think that was the most thoughtful, tender gift I've ever been given. I felt like we were little kids again. Whenever I felt alone, I'd pick up that stuffed animal—Adam's Curious George from his childhood—and hold it close. Curious George was a little worn, so I know he must have been valued and played with a lot as Adam grew up.

The security these friends offered to me was healing areas of pain that I didn't even suspect existed. All this attention opened me up like surgery. I began to experience all kinds of emotions. Adam and Jessica seemed to welcome them at first. I was quite overwhelmed, in fact. I've since learned that this experience is typical among those of us who begin to reveal this scary and confusing part of ourselves to others—allowing the first touches of genuine love in and letting our pain out. It's like opening the floodgates to emotions long since buried. Since we believe that we no longer have to pretend or conceal these feelings, they come out all at once. The emotions are delightful, scary, and painful all at the same time.

During the spring semester, as the acceptance and nonjudgmental attitude of my friends worked its magic within me, conflicting emotions began to emerge. First, I began to feel a crush toward Adam. When I first realized what the feeling was and put a name to it, I was terrified. I even felt a twinge of attraction toward Jessica! How confusing! Adam didn't take to either of these situations well.

I didn't know how to cope with these new feelings, so I kept them to myself. But Adam and Jessica both suspected. I didn't know what these thoughts or feelings meant. All I knew was that I felt evil for even having them. On the one hand, I felt badly about myself because I didn't want to feel infatuated with Adam; I felt like I was betraying him by having any romantic inclinations toward him and his girlfriend, Jessica. I felt so confused.

On the other hand, I had no control over these emotions. I've since learned that this confusion and feeling out of control is typical, too, among novice and even not-so-novice strugglers. The guilt I felt by being torn in two different directions took its toll on me, and I began to relate to Adam in unhealthy ways. I demanded too much of his attention. I wanted to talk about our problems all the time and seemed to be needy around him to an excessive degree. I realized how unhealthy it was, but I didn't know what to do.

Looking back I can see how my dependency developed, but I don't beat myself up about it like I used to. Though I was clumsy about it, I was trying hard to make sense of it all. Another man put it this way: "Although sexual attraction was there, the far deeper attraction was to finally be able to open up to another human being and be accepted and encouraged."[2] At least I could now say that one other man cared for me and knew all about me.

Because Adam and Jessica had made me feel safe, all of these feelings came forth like a tidal wave. They just kept coming out and coming out. I couldn't stop them. It felt both good and bad at the same time. I wanted to make sense of it. I needed to. Perhaps that's why I suffered so. My way of coping with my feelings was to overanalyze them.

In seeking help with homosexuality before college, I was taught to analyze emotional longings to find their source. This led to some nasty introspection. I applied this same technique to my friendships with Adam and Jessica; I analyzed what was wrong with me, what was wrong with them, and how we should "work on our relationship." This was a terrible mistake because it created a desertlike climate among the three of us.

One of the buildings on campus had a huge closet downstairs for storage. It was private and out-of-the-way, and had chairs inside to sit on. Adam, Jessica, and I met there one evening to talk (again!). A closet . . . how's that for unintentional irony? Adam had had enough. I remember his blunt words. He said, "I don't love you anymore as a friend." When I asked how this could be, he said, "It happens."

You could have knocked me over with a feather. He never wanted to see or speak to me again. He wished me well in my endeavors to sort through all the confusion in my life and said good-bye to me forever. No warnings. No options. No alternatives. Just good-bye. Jessica didn't talk to me after that, either. After the talk I felt light-headed. Trying to remember how to breathe, I staggered to my car.

I called, I wrote letters, but they were all ignored. The coldness coming from them as we passed in the hallways was unbearable. They wouldn't even make eye contact with me, and when I happened to approach or pass by them, they averted their eyes and walked the other way. I had to sit in a joint class with them twice a week. Can you imagine that? It was awful. My grades plummeted, and I lost interest in everything. If a person can be pummeled and still draw breath and walk around, that's how I felt for months following that evening meeting.

At the end of the semester, I received a note from Adam stating that he had nothing more to say to me and that I could pick up my possessions from the resident director. When I arrived, the RD told me that he knew about me because Adam had "confided" in him. We went upstairs, and I found all my stuff in a neat pile in the middle of the room with a note that said, "Thanks for the use of the items." Although it almost killed me, I asked the RD to return Curious George to Adam for me.

The inner lies about my insignificance returned with new force. How alone I felt, how ashamed and useless! Worse were the feelings of being unwanted and unwelcome—so unwelcome. People could tell that there was something terribly wrong, but no one knew what to say. I confided in a professor who now told me that the Christian college was not a good place for me and that I would be happier somewhere else. I felt awkward and estranged from the people who had been mutual friends of the three of us—me, Adam, and Jessica. I couldn't tell them what was going on without outing myself, so I felt ganged up on.

Once again, I began to believe the lies that I had worked so hard to break free from. With no sign that Adam and Jessica would re-think their attitude or behavior, I began to adopt the same attitude that they held toward me. Surely, if those whom I held in such high regard believed I deserved to be tossed aside like, as a friend put it, "used toilet paper," then I must have deserved it.

Adam was a leader on campus and represented the best of the college student body. If he reacted this way, others would too—right? Deeply shamed and feeling disgraced, I left the college for good.

Just when I thought I was going to totally lose my mind, my family helped me check into a hospital for the weekend under suicide watch. While I was there, something broke inside of me that may never mend. Everything I believed about God, the church, his people, homosexuality, and human nature turned on its ear. What a waste the previous months of joy seemed to be.

When I heard that I was "outed" to more than one individual there on campus, and God knows how many others, I felt desperately rejected and cut off. I had cold-sweat nightmares for months.

About a year later, someone encouraged me to reconcile with Adam and Jessica if possible, but they both refused to speak with me. This remains true to this day. I guess I just wanted to grasp at some straws of hope and find some measure of closure. I never got it. I've since heard that they think I lied to them and manipulated them into some kind of secret, homosexual agenda. How could Adam believe that I was after him *and* his girlfriend? Who convinced them that my feelings were planned, orchestrated, and contrived? They believe they treated me with respect and dignity and that the sharp break from me had been necessary.

My heart is not the only one that was broken from all of this. The event touched the lives of respected people on that campus including the college pastor, dean of students, professors, resident directors, and a host of other students, not to mention my friends and family. They dealt with the fallout.

Believe it or not, I still appreciate God. But I don't speak with him very much since the weekend in the hospital. For sure I don't understand or like the way he sometimes allows things in my life. I still appreciate his people, although I watch out and am careful and wary.

Although all who read my story here may not be open to learning about a homosexual friend or how to respond, some will be. I'm no longer a novice in the church's dealings with the homosexual. I know about homophobia. I know about misunderstanding, about love won and then love withdrawn.

Despite all that's happened and years of silence, I still care for Adam and Jessica. I don't know why, but I do. Sometimes I wish I didn't care for them because it hurts. I miss them. I've come to understand why they reacted the way they did, although I don't excuse them. I understand why I acted the way I did, yet I don't excuse myself, either. No one individual is to blame. I just wish we could forgive each other. I think of them and the experiences we shared with each other while in college.

Because I opened myself to them like no other before or since, they'll always have a special place in my heart. Before Adam left my life that night, I told him through my tears that no matter how he felt about me, I'd always be his friend. I meant it. I have kept my commitment and will not forget them even if we never reconcile. My memories of them have made for some restless days and sleepless nights, I assure you.

"Love the Lord your God with all your heart . . . love your neighbor as yourself" (Matt. 22:37–39). Jesus told us that this was the greatest commandment. After two thousand years of Christianity, this simple commandment sums up all he wants us to know and do. Stay committed to each other. Love each other unconditionally. Be with each other through the rough (even very rough) times and see it through. Christ-centered relationships are supposed to last. Don't turn your back on those who need you the most. You don't have to understand homosexuality in order to love someone.

I learned a lot at college. Like I said, I learned more than I ever could have imagined. Three years later, I was rummaging around in my parents' attic. Guess what I found? My own Curious George from when I was a boy.

Chew on It

1. Tom felt like he had to keep his struggle with same-sex attraction a secret. Have you ever tried to keep a secret? For how long? What made it hard to do?

2. Think of a time when you were embarrassed. What did you do to keep people from finding out what you had done?

3. Who do you turn to for comfort when you are anxious? What does that person do or say to ease your stress?

4. When Adam and Jessica first accepted Tom, he felt relief knowing he was no longer alone. When have you felt all alone? What circumstances caused you to feel lonely?

5. Even though many people were around him, Jesus felt all alone on the cross. In Matthew 27:46, he cried out, "My God, my God, why have you forsaken me?" How does Jesus' experience with loneliness help him understand how we feel?

2

What Do I Say . . . When Friends Tell Me They Are Gay?

When my friend Tom told his college buddies that he was gay, things went well at the beginning. His friends promised to stand by him and support him as he tried to move away from homosexuality. But somewhere along the line, fear replaced Adam and Jessica's desire to care for Tom. New emotions choked the friendship until it died.

How can you and I avoid these pitfalls with our friends who are gay?

Suppose one of your friends tells you that he or she is gay. Suddenly you realize that this person, the one you thought you knew, has been looking at the world from a radically different angle. How might *you* feel getting this news?

A common response is *shock*. In fact, some young people say they're gay just for shock value, to see how people react. But pause a moment. Look at your friend. Did a second head appear on his shoulder? Did her skin erupt with green spots? No? Then this is still the person you've always known. You're just learning a new dimension of who that person is.

Maybe your friend is a Christian. You ask, "How could a Christian have feelings like these?" Answer? Christians grapple with every issue in the books: depression, anorexia, drugs . . . and homosexuality. That's reality. Being baptized doesn't exempt a person from Life 101.

Fear is another natural reaction. What does this mean in our friendship? Will people think I'm gay if we're seen together? Will my friend come on to me? Whoa! Just being the same sex as your gay friend does not mean that he or she will come on to you. Because a guy is gay, it doesn't mean that every male turns him on. Because a lesbian has a cup of coffee with another female, it doesn't mean she's sexually aroused. As a firmly heterosexual woman, I'm not excited by every male who walks by my desk. The movie star that ignites heart palpitations in one woman may cause me to yawn. Likewise, your gay friend may not perceive you as a sexual target at all.

When you learn that someone you know is gay, you might respond with *anger*. You may feel betrayed or hurt because for months or years your friend has hidden away in a pocket a key piece to a puzzle. The friend didn't put all the cards on the table. Be careful if you're angry. You may say words you'll later regret. One mother I know discovered her son was gay and wrote a flaming letter condemning him. Fortunately she spoke with my husband before she headed to the post office, and he urged her not to mail the letter. A short time after that, the son died. The mother thanked us that she had not cut off her relationship with the son in that first fit of passion.

Another emotion you might feel when you hear your friend has same-sex desires may be *denial*. If I don't think about it, it isn't there. Some people offer this advice as a "cure" for their gay friends. Ignore it, and the feeling will go away. But it doesn't work. Let me give you an example from a different arena.

One November, a large woman came into my office for a pregnancy test. I began to fill out the paperwork. "How long has it been since your last period?"

"Nine months," she replied.

Nine months! Thinking she had misunderstood me, I asked again, "When did you last have a period?"

"February," she answered.

Thanksgiving vacation was the following week! For nine months this woman had refused to accept that she was pregnant. I discovered that she'd come to my office directly from the hospital, where they'd treated her for prelabor pains. And now she wanted a pregnancy test?

Her pregnancy did not go away simply because she refused to think about it. Nor will homosexual feelings pack their bags and leave on their own. If a same-sex friend has mustered the courage to confide in you, it's likely your friend has been thinking for a long time about these feelings. Those feelings are not going to go away by ignoring them.

When someone tells you he or she is gay, you may feel *overwhelmed*. This feeling is often followed by the question, "How do I fix this problem?" Relax! *You* can't. You're the friend, and your job is to support your friend as he or she works through the choices ahead: Will he act on his feelings? Will she try to change?

Several years ago in the cartoon strip *For Better or For Worse*, the character Mike learned that Lawrence, one of his best friends, was gay. Mike's first reaction was shock and denial: he says, "I won't believe it!" Lawrence protests that it isn't as if he chose to be gay! He wants to be like everyone else. He stares at Mike, hoping for a word of comfort, but Mike reacts with fear, saying, "Why are you looking at me like that?" He thinks his friend might be coming on to him. Lawrence explains, "You're my friend, Mike! There's a big difference between friends and lovers . . . and right now I really need a friend."

Help! I'm in Crisis!

Shock, fear, anger, denial, stress. These are the same emotions that people experience when they face a major crisis such as a death in the family or loss of a job. Or when a man discovers he has cancer or a woman learns her house has burned down. Why would the news that a friend is gay put us into crisis mode? Because it threatens our sense of order. We thought we knew this person, and suddenly we find we didn't know him or her at all.

The word *crisis* comes from a Greek word that means "turning point." Think of a basketball player holding the ball on the court. The player pivots this way . . . turns that way. To whom will the player pass the ball? He or she must make a decision.

Even a decision not to decide is still a decision. Say, for example, that a rock is falling from a cliff above your head. You have to decide whether to stay put or to move. If you can't decide, you may get hurt because whether you make a choice or not, the rock will continue to fall. Or again, remember that pregnant woman who came into my office and refused to believe she was pregnant? Suppose she couldn't decide whether to abort her child or carry to term. Hasn't she made a decision by default? Not deciding means she'll carry to term because the pregnancy won't simply disappear. Likewise, if she can't decide whether to parent or place for adoption, she's made a choice to parent, because the baby won't find an adoptive home on its own.

When a friend tells you he or she is gay, you're at a "turning point" in your relationship. Will you abandon ship or will you stay around?

The Chinese character for the word *crisis* is a composite of two symbols, sort of like a hyphenated word. One means "opportunity," while the other character represents "danger." When put together, the two symbols become one and mean "opportunity riding on a dangerous wind." Often, when we're in crisis mode, all we see is the danger around us. Our world order is threatened. Things look like they'll fall apart. We respond with shock or fear. We have to learn to cope by developing new skills—skills that are awkward and untested.

But a crisis is more than a threat. It is also an opportunity. When your friend tells you he or she is gay, your friendship has an opportunity to grow in new directions. Let's not lose sight of that opportunity.

Shock, fear, anger, denial, stress. After your friend gives you "the news," imagine you ran out of the room, screaming, "Help! Help!" How would your friend feel? Rejected? Abandoned? Suppose your cousin tells you she's a lesbian, and you try to change the subject or you immediately try to fix her. How does she feel? Trivialized? Put down? Will either of these people ever again approach you for help?

Shock, fear, anger, denial, stress. All these are negative emotions. May I suggest another response? A positive one? Be *glad*! Be glad your friend trusts you with his or her secret. It took time for that trust to grow. This person has probably observed you for weeks or even months, wondering if you're a "safe" person to share this most private secret. Be glad! You passed the test. Your friend trusts you.

So what do you say to your friend who's gay? Try the words: "Thanks for trusting me!"

Can We Still Be Friends?

You may wonder if you can still be friends with them. In a word . . . yes! Gays need friends just as you and I need friends. They need people who'll support them, pray for them, and help them sort through the tangle of their thoughts. Instead of tossing gay friends aside, perhaps we should come alongside them and offer help. Today, having real friends is more important than ever. Skyrocketing divorce rates, promiscuous sex, and broken hearts all indicate that many people—not just gays—need help with relationships.

I read about a man who faced a crisis. He lost everything he had. His business went bankrupt. Vandals trashed his house. His children died in a freak accident. His own brothers and sisters avoided him like a cracked mirror. Then he got cancer. People crossed the street when they saw him coming for fear his bad luck would be contagious. Out of all his friends, only three stuck around.

These were extraordinary friends, however. Though they didn't live near him, they dropped everything to rush to his side. They each took off over a week from work, left their own families, and traveled to be near their friend when he most needed them. They grieved with him. They waited until he was able to talk, and then they helped him face his fears. They didn't always say the right things—in all honesty, some things they said were just plain wrong and hurt deeply—but they stayed by him for the whole ride. That's why when the crisis passed, this man, a guy named Job, was able to forgive them for those painful moments. He trusted that they had done their best to help.[1]

How do you find friends like that? Can you go on eBay and order one that fits your needs? Or do you look at résumés on Monster .com and interview each person who applies?

In chapter 1, Tom described his friendship with Adam. When they first met, Tom was attracted by superficial features. "Adam awed me from day one. His athletic prowess and even the way he carried himself impressed me so much. He thought nothing of joining the college basketball team for a pickup game, playing soccer or hockey with the guys on the floor, and always returning to the room sweaty and invigorated. *That's what real men do*, I thought, and I wished I had the skills to do that." Envy is not a strong foundation for a healthy friendship.

Tom got to know Adam better. "Handsome and charming, Adam had no difficulty winning friends—the kind of friends I wanted. So much about him challenged me. I watched him closely and believed that I could learn a lot from him. He was popular, confident, and secure in his identity as a man. I sensed so much masculine power in him. A guy like that wanted to hang with me? Wow!"

Yet, as Tom soon learned, looks and social connections aren't enough to hold a friendship together.

So what does hold two friends together? I once asked a college class to tell me what characteristics they valued most in their friends. Here's a partial list of their answers:

- Honesty
- Loyalty
- Commitment

- Sense of humor
- Vulnerability
- Similar interests
- Compassion
- Respect
- Kindness
- Empathy
- Confidentiality
- Hospitality
- Caring
- Encouraging
- Trusting
- Gentleness
- Patience
- Dependability
- Loving
- Understanding
- Able to give and take in the relationship

Whether I'm talking with young people from affluent suburbs or kids from inner-city streets, the list is the same. Tall, short, curly hair or not, people give the same answers. It doesn't matter whether the person is gay or straight. Each of us yearns for deep friendships.

Nobody puts "heterosexual" or "homosexual" on the list of qualities. Why? Because sexual orientation is not the most important element in determining whether a friendship will fly. Look at that list. How many of those qualities listed involve physical intimacy? Sure, we all long for the occasional hug, the pat on the back. But deep friendships, above all, require communication. Which of the qualities on the list does not include a verbal component? How can anyone be vulnerable without sharing one's inmost thoughts? What is honesty without words? How can you have compassion without saying, "Can I help?"

The essential elements in a strong friendship don't revolve

around whether your friend is gay or straight. The essentials involve trust, honesty, and respect.

Important qualities like the ones listed above don't appear overnight. You discover them over time. My mother once told me that if a person had five close friends in the course of a lifetime, that person could consider himself or herself rich.

My mother's best friendships took decades to develop. That's why she struggled when my dad changed jobs a few years before he retired. After living in California for many years, they moved across the country. Then they moved three more times in a five-year span. My mother left behind in California people who had walked with her through the anguish of losing two babies at birth. Her friends had sat with her at baptisms and graduations. These friends had played jokes on each other. Now as she faced retirement, my mother grieved because she realized there weren't enough years left in her life to develop roots in her new location, deep roots that would result in friendships like the ones she'd left behind in California.

Don't expect to find fine wine at a fast-food counter. Developing a fine friendship takes time. And if you have an awesome friend, and that friend later reveals to you that he or she is gay, this is not the time to discard that friend. Healthy friendships involve accepting the other person as he or she really is. A friend is not a project to work on, to transform into something that meets your needs or expectations, not even if that friend turns out to be gay.

Hand Me Some Superglue!

Friends can be like sandpaper, smoothing off the rough edges of our personalities. My husband and I are forever grateful to our college roommates who put up with us before we married. I don't mean these people tried to change us. But we saw new dimensions of ourselves reflected in these relationships. I still treasure a letter from a quiet roommate who had courage to tell me that I intimidated her. She valued our friendship enough to risk telling me the truth.

Have you dreamed about having a friend—someone who is dependable and trustworthy? Suppose that person possessed all the qualities you dreamed of and then confessed that he or she struggled with same-sex attraction. Why would you reject all that person's positive qualities in order to hang a neon sign around his or her neck that shouted, "Gay! Gay! Gay!"?

Making a choice to stick by a friend, gay or not, distinguishes true friendship from brother/sister relationships. In a family, you have no choice about your brothers and sisters. They come with the territory. For better or for worse, you're stuck with each other. Strong friendships, though, require social superglue. Long ago, college fraternities and sororities tried to pattern themselves after family relationships. *Frater* means "brother" and *soror* means "sister." When a person decides to pledge a fraternity or sorority, they enter into an intentional grouping. They're supposed to be as loyal to their friends in the fraternity as they would be to flesh and blood siblings.

You don't need to join a fraternity or sorority to have a loyal friend. All you need to do is decide to work on the friendships you already have. Like a relationship with a brother or sister, a friendship will change and mature over time. The friend who is gay or lesbian, the one you wondered how to respond to, may become the very person who later holds *you* up in a storm.

Pain with the Gain

Friendship always costs us something. It may involve sacrificing time, adjusting priorities, giving up resources. It may hurt.

People have let me down. A longtime friend of mine once borrowed a large sum of money, then, through no fault of his own, went bankrupt and failed to repay the loan. At the time I asked myself, *Is this friendship worth more than the thousand bucks I'm out?* I decided it would cost far more to start over and build a new friendship with someone else.

Steve met Ron in a cancer support group. Ron had colon cancer, and twice he had operations to remove parts of his colon. Then the cancer spread to his liver. They removed sections of it. A few years later, the disease spread to his lungs, and they removed the lower lobe of the lung. Ron used to say, "Steve, I'm going to heaven . . . a little bit of me at a time." Then Ron died.

Steve attended the funeral. "It would be very easy to draw a wrong conclusion from this experience . . . a conclusion, unfortunately, that many people make. They make the conclusion, 'If you don't get close, you won't get hurt.' After all, friends die. They develop other relationships. Friends let us down. They hurt us deeply. If you don't let them get close, they can't hurt you. If you don't get close, you may experience the absence of pain, but you also experience the absence of living. My life is far richer for having known Ron despite the pain of losing him."

When your friend tells you about a struggle with same-sex attraction, you can look for the nearest exit or stick around and dig for buried treasure.

How Would Christ Respond to Gays?

Who were the people tossed aside by society when Jesus walked on earth? The tax collectors, the lame, the prostitutes, the lepers, the orphans, the widows. All were pushed to the margins of the social register. How did Jesus respond to these people? He reached out to them and drew them in.

If Jesus reached out to these people long ago, would he turn away from those whom our society rejects? Today, he would extend his arms to the single mom, the AIDS victim, the homeless, the person strung out on drugs, and . . . yes . . . the gays and lesbians. He might even embrace the skinhead or white supremacist!

Did Jesus face consequences? When people saw him with "that type," his reputation was at stake. Sometimes being seen with a prostitute was awkward, or healing a leper was inconvenient. So why did he take the risk? Because he cared about these individuals. And he calls us to do the same.

Remember Tom's friends, Adam and Jessica, who discarded him like used toilet paper? When Adam severed their friendship, Tom said, "The weight of his rejection pinned me to my chair and my mind clouded over. I waited for Adam and Jessica to take it all back, to say they didn't mean it. I searched in their eyes for the friends I'd come to know so well, the friends who promised me unconditional love—but they were gone."

Instead of that picture of a discarded piece of toilet paper, substitute a different idea. Imagine a plaster cast. Your arm is broken, and it hurts! The doctor sets the arm and puts it in a cast. Weeks pass, and the bone eventually heals. The bone becomes stronger than it was before.

Friendships may break under stress, but they can heal too. The initial injury is painful. Perhaps trust is ripped in half. There is anger. Anger is a symptom that something is out of whack in the spirit just as pain indicates something is wrong in the physical body.

Like a broken bone, trust can be restored. Someone has to say, "I'm sorry," and the other person needs to forgive. Healing requires commitment, which acts like a plaster cast, holding two people together while the friendship heals. Healing takes time—sometimes a long time—but when two people work through their differences, the final bond becomes stronger than ever. Those friends can be gay or straight. My friend Tom needed a friend like that.

Chew on It

1. Think about three people you call friends. Would you have named the same people five years ago? List some of the shared experiences that initially drew you together.

2. What personal characteristics draw you to each of your friends? What qualities appear on all three lists? If one of your friends were gay, how would that fact affect these qualities?

3. Have you ever lost contact with a friend? What caused the friendship to end?

4. If you had contact with that person today, would you do anything different now? What?

5. What do you think it means when the Bible says, "As iron sharpens iron, a friend sharpens a friend" (Prov. 27:17)?

3

What Do I Say . . . When Someone Hints Those Guys Are Gay?

"Nate," "Jason," and the other individuals who introduce the following chapters in this book are real people. Their names, as well as certain details in the story they tell, have been changed to protect their true identities. Though you may find the story hard to believe, the events described here really happened. The father did attempt to kill his son's best friend. And people still argue whether the two young men were gay. Now it's your turn to decide. Walk into police headquarters, sneak into Nate's office, and meet these young men for yourself. What do you think?

Nate, what's with your dad?" Jason demanded.

"What do you mean? I just saw him in his office. He seemed fine then."

"I can't figure the guy out. One moment he's my good buddy, the next time he's giving me the cold hardly-know-you shoulder. How long have you and I known each other, Nate? Over two years? Your dad introduced us, for Pete's sake. He seemed excited when I began spending serious time with your family. Christmas, Easter—your dad wanted me there at the table eating with the aunts, uncles, kids."

"So what's your point?"

"Well, now he's giving off all these mixed signals. Last week he has a headache, right? He asks me to get my guitar and play some funky Simon and Garfunkel tune from the 1960s, says it's 'easy listening' and will make his headache go away. But after a few minutes, he explodes and tells me to get lost! So okay, he's not feeling well. But on the weekend, I'm just standing there talking to your sister Micki in the front hall when your dad glares at me and tells me to leave!"

"He's getting a lot of pressure at work, Jason."

"Yeah? Well, that's another thing. It might not be so bad if we didn't all work at the same place, but having your dad as my boss is really putting some major stress on me. I'm thinking maybe it's time to be moving on, finding some place else to work."

"No way! You can't be serious!"

"Nate, this has been going on longer than you realize. I didn't want to say anything 'cause . . . after all . . . he's your father, but things are getting worse every day. I'm not talking about minor stuff. Yesterday he wrote up a formal reprimand for me. Here I was supposed to be up for another promotion, and now he's threatening to fire me? Am I his personal yo-yo? What's going on?"

"Jason, cool it. Don't do anything stupid. Just lay low for a week or so while I find out what's up."

After Jason left, Nate shook his head and leaned back in his chair. Nate knew there'd been tension between his dad and Jason but things were getting worse in a hurry. Nate had known Jason for only a couple of years, yet they felt like brothers. Nate had already been a member of the metropolitan police force for several years, and his father, Kyle, was the police commissioner when Jason joined the force as a rookie cop. Normally, an experienced cop like Nate and a newbie like Jason wouldn't have crossed paths in such a huge department, except for a fluke event.

A man named Matthew Iron led a radical neo-Nazi group. For

six months Iron had been at the top of the FBI's most wanted list after killing three agents in a shoot-out. After escaping a nationwide
hunt, Iron showed up in the metro area. Nate's father sent a couple
of cops to search for him in the warehouse district. Only Iron found
them first. The skinhead had the cops pinned in an alley against a
wall. And who shows up? Jason. He wasn't on duty. No uniform to
identify him as a cop. No weapons. Not even a Kevlar vest for protection. He just happened to walk around the corner from the next
alley, right into the barrel of Iron's 8mm semiautomatic.

Faster than a junkie fleeing a drug bust, Jason grabbed a fire escape above his head and swung his feet into the air. One foot caught
the barrel of the Uzi and sent the weapon flying. The other foot
landed on Iron's head. It all took place in a breath. Iron collapsed to
the ground. When the other cops came running, weapons drawn,
they discovered Iron dead. One minute he'd been threatening their
lives, the next he lay at their feet stone dead.

After that episode, the whole world knew Jason. All over the
country his face appeared on magazine covers and flashed across
TV screens. Talk shows fought each other to get rights to interview
him. And Jason was, of course, ushered into the office of the head
of the metropolitan police force. Kyle took pride in knowing that
one of his men had caught Iron. He took Jason home to meet the
family. Jason met Nate there, the two guys hit it off and, as they say,
the rest is history.

So why was Kyle turning against Jason? Nate grabbed a pencil
from his desk drawer and began weaving it in and out, back and
forth between his fingers. Nothing made sense. His father used to
be a calm guy, never raising his voice. In fact, when Nate was a kid
and first learned to shoot a gun, Kyle told him, "Son, never shoot
when you're angry. It affects your aim. You'll miss the target, and
in a shoot-out, that can mean life or death."

For years, Nate had looked up to his father, idolizing him. Of
course everyone had to look up to him. Kyle stood tall, taller than
anyone in the department. His shoes, his shirts, his slacks all had
to be special ordered because nothing that was standard issue

would fit. Now Nate had grown almost as tall as his father. Before the events of 9–11, people had sometimes called the two men the Twin Towers. Nate would laugh, saying, "Dad's more like the Sears Tower! He's a good deal taller than me!"

Still, there had been cracks in the foundation. Last month Nate had stopped by his dad's office to drop off a report and heard him yelling at one of the secretaries. Kyle had grabbed the doorknob and ripped it right off the door. Nate wouldn't have believed it if he hadn't seen it with his own eyes. And then there was the time his father got upset over some missing crime scene evidence. He slugged a wall and punched a hole in it the size of his fist.

Yes, something was gnawing there under the public facade that Kyle showed at press conferences. Nate decided to ask his mother for her thoughts when he walked into the house that evening.

"Hi, Mom! What's for dinner?"

His mother looked up at her son with pride. To think this man had once been a babe in her arms! "When did you get to be so tall?" she asked, as she wrapped her arms around his waist.

"I don't know. When did you get to be so small?" Nate smiled.

"Grab some carrots there and start peeling. I've got pot roast in the oven."

Nate reached for the cutting board and pulled a carrot peeler from the drawer. He nibbled on a freshly washed green bean from the strainer in the sink.

"Hey, those are for supper. Hands off!"

Nate grinned and raised his arms above his head. "Caught me! I give up!"

His mother punched him lightly in the belly. "That'll do. What brings you by? I thought you were too busy fixing up your car to have time to stop by and see your mother."

"Come on. Don't make it sound like I never visit. I came here last Sunday."

"Right. Because Micki told you we were having curried chicken. So what's on your mind?"

"Mom, does Dad ever get angry at you?"

"Angry?! Now what ever made you ask that? No, he's pretty even-keeled. For years he never even shouted at me. Pretty amazing. He's gotten angry at other people, but never at me or at one of you kids . . . though you gave him lots of reasons to explode . . . like when you left his car in neutral and it rolled down the hill and hit the Williamsons' garage. No, he's a pretty calm guy. He might let his temper fly at the office, but he'd never hurt anyone he loves."

"That makes sense. Thanks. It just seems like he's upset at Jason, and it's good to know that Dad wouldn't hurt him."

After dinner, Nate stopped by headquarters once more on his way back to his apartment. The light glowed in Jason's office. Nate poked his head in at the door.

"Missed you at dinner. Mom served pot roast and fresh apple pie."

Jason looked up and shook his head. Nate immediately became serious. He noticed Jason's fingers tightly gripping the edge of the desk. Nate grabbed a chair, swung it around, and straddled the seat.

"I don't plan on eating that apple pie again for a while," Jason said. "Not for a long time."

"What happened? *Mom's* not mad at you!"

"No, but your father is. Want to know why? My guess is he's jealous."

"Jealous!"

"Listen up, Nate. Here's my theory. After all that business about Matthew Iron, your father couldn't handle it. After all, the switchboard went nuts with everyone calling in to ask about me, to interview me, to get my photo. It upset him that a rookie cop was known all over the country when he himself had worked for years to get to the top of the heap. People have hinted that he's also upset that you and I spend so much time together. He's used to being your idol. Maybe he thinks I've displaced him there, too."

"You're telling me that a man—commissioner of the whole force, thirty years of experience, a résumé six pages long, a name recognized all over the state—is feeling threatened by someone who's been in the department for only a couple of years?"

"There's more, if you'd keep quiet. Seems like there are some rumors going around about you and me."

"Rumors? About us? What do you mean?"

"You know . . . rumors. People are whispering that we're around each other all the time, that it's not normal for two guys to hang around together as much as we do, that we're . . ."

"We're what? Cut the small talk."

"You know . . . like we're . . . more than friends."

"Aw, come on! Gay? *Gay*! You've gotta be kidding! People think we're *gay*?"

"Shut up, Nate! Saying something doesn't make it true."

"Jason, look at me! Do I look *gay* to you?" Nate struck a martial arts pose.

"Stop it! You're crazy! You can't tell if someone's gay just by looking at them. What I'm saying is that the rumors add fuel to the fire. If your father plays the rumors right, he can get rid of me and get his son back."

"Jason, you're the one who's crazy. I just talked to my mom. She assured me that Dad would never hurt someone he loved. You're part of the family. You're like a son to him. He wouldn't touch you!"

"Oh yeah? I stopped by your place earlier this afternoon, dropping off those apples that you ate in the pie. I went down to the family room and was playing my guitar when your father came in and screamed at me to stop! He ripped the guitar from my hands, stomped across the room, and, just when he was about to bash it against the wall, he turned around and hurled it at me. If I hadn't ducked, this body would be seriously hurting. Then he came at me again. That's when I cut out. Not even a dog would stay near someone acting like that!"

"You're telling me Dad actually attacked you?"

"Assault? Battery? Yeah, those words fit."

"Jason, this is my father we're talking about! I've got to . . ."

"Whatever you do, you're on your own, bro, because I'm laying low. Next time this body is in the same room with that man, I'm wearing a flak jacket!"

Chew on It

1. How would you feel if your father tried to hurt your best friend?

2. What possible reasons can you think of to explain why your dad might want to hurt your friend?

3. How far would you go to protect your friend's life?

4. What does the following statement say about friendship?

   Here is how to measure [love]—the greatest love is shown when people lay down their lives for their friends. (John 15:13)

4

What Do I Say . . . When I'm Not Sure If My Friend Is Gay?

WHEN JASON TOLD ME about the rumors that we were gay and that Dad had attacked him, his story blew me away. What would make my own father think such a thing? Let's be real. Dad is a police officer! He's trained to get the facts. Sure, Dad gets angry. Sure, he's even hit things when he was upset. But there's a big difference between slugging a wall and attacking a person.

I wanted to trust my father, but I also knew Jason was telling the truth. After all, he's my best friend. We're like wheels on a motorcycle, always working together. Nobody's ever known Jason to exaggerate, let alone tell a lie.

Hearing that Dad had attacked Jason was like seeing a freak tornado blow into my world and twist it beyond recognition. Until that day, I'd always respected my father. Then . . . boom! I learned about a side of my dad I never knew existed. It was like discovering your father has left the family and gone off with another woman. Like he suddenly had another family that lived in a parallel universe. Where's the guy who took me fishing and taught me to throw a football? Who was this new guy?

That's when I tried to talk to Dad myself. Instead of apologizing, he got angry at ME! He told me, "Nate! Don't you realize I had to do this for you? You think you'll ever get to be a commissioner like me if people think you're gay? As long as Jason's in the picture? No way!"

I had to walk out of the room to avoid knocking him flat. For the first time I realized I'd inherited the same temper as Dad. I steered clear of him until we both calmed down. I hunted for Jason and found him staring at a cup of cold coffee in the diner across from headquarters.

"Jason, he must be crazy! My brain's flown through a blender trying to sort through this. There's got to be an explanation. Who started these rumors? You're saying all this stuff began a few weeks ago? But you just got engaged to my sister. Explain that, huh? Dad didn't object to you marrying Micki."

That's when it hit me. Maybe Jason was right. Maybe Dad did worry about Jason being my best friend. Maybe Dad thought that Jason really was gay or that Micki would distract Jason from paying attention to me.

"Jason," I asked, "how can people think you're gay if you're marrying my sister?"

"Nate, people say the engagement is a cover-up. Lots of gay guys marry girls. Some think it will solve their problems. Others marry just to stop talk. I'm not gay. Tell me you believe that, don't you? Even if I were gay, I'd never hurt your sister by pretending. I told you already—I love Micki. But people still talk."

"Jason, what do we do? I know how to arrest a thief and read him his rights. I know how to take down a mugger. But how do you fight talk?"

In an earlier chapter, we assumed that a friend of yours came to you and told you about how he or she struggled with same-sex attraction. But what if your friend hasn't said anything of the sort? What do you do if someone starts a rumor that your friend is gay? How do you know if it's true? And what if people whisper that you're both gay? As Nate said, "How do you fight talk?"

Being single is tough these days. If two girls head to the beach for the day, they naturally help each other put on sunscreen, smoothing it over those hard to reach spots on the back. But will two guys help each other smear sunscreen on? They'd rather burn! Someone might see them and think they were gay!

Think about living arrangements. If you share a room with someone of the same sex, people assume you're gay. If you live alone, you're clearly a misfit and can't get along with anyone. If you hang around someone of the opposite sex, people think you're sleeping together.

People all around you talk. People at school, at work, even at church. Recently I ran into a young woman who graduated from the college where my husband teaches. Martha and a girlfriend were sharing an apartment. As new graduates who had school loans to pay off, the two girls figured they could cut expenses by living together. Now, though they get along well, Martha wonders if sharing an apartment was a smart idea. She's seen people look at them sideways. At church she's heard murmurs, "Are they lesbians?"

Another friend of mine is upset. On two occasions his classmates have taunted him, calling him names. He asks, "What have I done to make them think I'm gay?" Just because people whisper that someone is gay doesn't mean it's true.

No one is immune from rumors. Two single friends of mine, two gray-haired women who are in their seventies, have shared a home for over three decades. When they hit the thirty-year mark, they thought about inviting people to an anniversary celebration, but Esther told me, "We were concerned about what people would think." How sad that they were unable to celebrate so many years of friendship for fear of rumors.

When I first arrived at college, I had a roommate I'd never met before. After a month or two living with me, my roommate told someone she thought I was a lesbian. Her reason? I wrote "Love you!" at the bottom of phone messages I left on her desk. If, though, she'd opened up my correspondence with a hundred other people—including my parents, brothers, and male friends—she would have found the same phrase attached to their letters.

Because of the potential for misunderstandings and rumors, some young people bypass same-sex friendships altogether. Those ordinary friendships, however, are the training ground for future dating and marriage relationships. Same-sex friendships teach us how to communicate, how to trust, and how to support each other without the additional complexity of sexual intimacy.

How Do Rumors Get Started?

Lots of emotions lie at the root of rumors.

In the case of my roommate, it turned out that, a week before coming to school, she'd broken off her engagement to a young man. She was supersensitive about the meaning of those words "Love you!" Her personal pain resulted in misinterpreting my words.

Sometimes a rumor begins when one person is angry at another person. A guy I'll call "Abe" hurt his friend "Dave." As a result, Dave refused to speak to Abe for over seven years. In frustration, Abe began a whisper campaign that almost ruined Dave's reputation.

Perhaps one person will benefit if another person is torn down. When Abe got Dave in trouble, Abe also went after Dave's job. It meant a big raise in salary.

Maybe the rumor stems from jealousy. "Carlos" and "Paul" were friends for several years. They met at work and discovered they attended the same church. They both enjoyed golf, and they went on a trip together. But when Paul wanted to spend time with his other friends, Carlos couldn't handle it. Rather than admit that he felt threatened by Paul's other friends, Carlos started a rumor that Paul was gay.

Hurt, anger, jealousy, and ambition are like manure that feeds the roots of rumors. But sometimes none of these are involved. Sometimes people don't know the truth about a friendship. They see you consistently hanging out with the same friend, and they make assumptions based on a hurried observation: "They must be gay."

People Make Wrong Assumptions

It hurts when people make assumptions about you without getting to know you. I often counsel young people facing unplanned pregnancies. You might ask, "What on earth does a girl having a baby have to do with rumors about being gay?" Well, a lot of people talk when a single girl gets pregnant. And like you and your friend, these young couples who come into my office have feelings. They feel hurt when someone presumes to know what's going on in their relationship.

Imagine, for example, the young man who discovers that his girlfriend is pregnant. He tells his friends that he plans to marry her. If they say, "You're going to marry her? Her father must be putting a lot of pressure on you!" the young man may become defensive. They've assumed that he wouldn't marry the girl if he had a choice.

On the other hand, maybe the girl tells her teacher that she's not going to marry the father of her baby. If the teacher replies, "Oh, your boyfriend dumped you as soon as he found out you were pregnant," the girl feels judged. Her boyfriend may still be in the picture and want to marry her, but for other reasons she's decided not to rush into marriage. She could accuse the teacher, "You made no effort to find out the truth."

By the way, even pregnant women aren't safe from assumptions about being gay. "Stacy," expecting her first baby, struggled financially as a single mom. Common sense would tell you that Stacy, being pregnant, must have been sexually active with a man, right? But when Stacy's friend "Brianne" moved in to help her share the expenses of an apartment, people wondered if the girls were lesbians.

If people raise their eyebrows when they see you with someone of the same sex and suggest that you're both gay, the problem may not reflect wrong behavior on your part. Rather, people may not know you. Lack of knowledge leads to lack of trust. So if someone whispers that a friend of yours might be gay, don't assume that the rumor is true. The first step is to get the facts.

Maria told me about two men who worked at her company. One of them was very sensitive and soft spoken, a poet. The two men always sat very close together, and at times one would put his arm around the other. "At first I was uncomfortable," said Maria, "and I saw that some other people were uncomfortable, too."

Maria began by stereotyping: he's a poet, therefore he must be gay. But then she got to know one of the men better. "We opened our home to him and he'd just come and chat, drop in for a meal. Then he left to get married, and the other guy went to the wedding and was his best man."

Then Maria got to know the second guy. "He, too, would drop in for a video or tea, or whatever; we even had a combined birthday party together."

Shortly after this, the second young man also got married. Maria thought, "I'm so glad I didn't let their special friendship obstruct my getting to know these guys!" She knew that there's a very thin line between a real close friendship and a friendship that's maybe too close. Sometimes there may be a weakness in one or the other that causes the friendship to fall apart because of rumors, but these guys knew each other well enough so as not to be threatened. And what's more, they didn't let the questioning looks of others hinder their friendship.

Not Only Sticks and Stones Hurt!

Rumors can have horrible consequences. Rumors have overturned governments. They escalate strife between family members or co-workers. They separate friends. They generate fear and distrust. Rumors create confusion. The author of a rumor doesn't put his name on it so you don't know whom to trust. And innocent people get hurt.

Remember I mentioned Carlos, who hinted that his friend Paul might be gay? Paul felt betrayed when he heard the rumor. After all, Paul had sounded the original alarm about the friendship. He had sensed things were too intense and tried to back off and spend more time seeing other friends. Then Paul's wife heard the rumor. She didn't know whom to believe. She loved Paul, but it took months of marriage counseling to undo the damage caused by Carlos's careless words.

What If I Suspect My Friend Is Gay?

Maybe your friend hasn't told you that he or she is gay. You're only guessing. I asked a girl how she knew if someone in a crowd was gay. She said she looked to see whether the guy had a slender build, if he had jewelry on his hands, and . . . if he had a habit of text messaging!

Let's begin by discarding stereotypes. The picture of the gay guy as having a limp handshake and feminine features is a far cry from reality. Ditto for the lesbian as having large muscles and a butch haircut. "Theo" is a handsome college guy who has broad shoulders and V-shaped torso. He's outgoing, has a great sense of humor . . . and he's gay.

If you think your friend is gay, but he or she hasn't told you about it, professional counselors say don't bring it up. Despite your best intentions, you may do more damage than good. Asking about a person's sexual orientation may cause that person to question his or her identity. They may think, *If my friend thinks I'm gay, maybe I am.*

It could be that your friend is confused about homosexuality. Your friend may not be sure whether he or she is gay. Bisexuals, for example, may alternate between male and female partners, first disappointed by one sex, then hurt by the other. A person's confusion in regard to sexual preferences may not, in fact, revolve around whom he or she *wants* as a partner (male or female) but who that person *is* (his or her own identity). Some people, because of confusion about their own identities, can't relate well to either sex.

Don't bring up the question "Are you gay?" but do be available to talk. You might, for example, be watching a sitcom on TV at your friend's house. The plot revolves around a topic like gay marriage. The comments you make in response to the program can open or close a conversation with your friend. If you gripe about pushy gays and their political agenda, you slam the door shut. If you snicker and use slang terms to describe the characters in the program, your friend will never trust you with his or her personal questions about sexual identity. When you dislike a sitcom, a car, even a meal, and say "That's so gay!" be aware of the impact that phrase has on someone who struggles with same-sex attraction.

For that matter, while you're at the Dumpster tossing out stereotypes of gays and getting rid of negative vocabulary, discard any jokes about gays. You never know who's listening at the next table. Gays will never approach you for help after hearing you laugh at their expense.

One more caution: Don't ask a third party whether your friend might be gay. That's how rumors take off!

How Do You Stop a Rumor?

Have you ever been in the locker room at the gym and heard a story about someone you knew?

"Did you hear about . . . ?"

"I couldn't believe he would do such a thing!"

"Could it be true? I saw them together at . . ."

Before you pass the story along, pause a moment. The more people who pass along a rumor, the more that rumor is likely to be believed. A wise man once said, "Fire goes out for lack of fuel, and quarrels disappear when gossip stops" (Prov. 26:20).

The simplest way to stop a rumor is to shut your mouth. Don't pass it on. Let it die.

"Yes," you say, "but other people keep it going."

You're right. So the next step is to find out the truth. Don't assume a rumor about a friend being gay has any basis in fact until you've done some homework.

Get to the source. Make an effort to talk to your friend. Listen. Get a handle on his or her perspective. Even in court you're presumed innocent until proven guilty. Give the object of the rumor a chance to defend himself or herself! If the rumor were about you, wouldn't you want a chance to set the record straight?

What If the Rumor Is About Me?

Suppose the person they're talking about is *you*. You're in the library but a wall of books stands between you and the people on the other side. You overhear snickering. You hear your name. They're talking about you and your best friend.

They think you're both gay.

Maybe your face turns red. Perhaps your heart beats faster. Your fist clenches. Before you punch the speaker, pause again.

Who is the speaker? Is it someone you know? Would you have believed this individual if he or she had been talking about someone else?

Ask yourself, *Is there a shred of evidence that could support this case? What's the basis of this rumor?*

Self-examination is a healthy process. Maybe it is time to stand back and look at your friendship through the eyes of other people. While you may not have crossed a boundary into homosexuality, you may have spent a lot of time alone with one friend and excluded others. If two guys have been working together on a special project for a class, perhaps a simple explanation would clear the air. "Yeah, it's true that Josh and I have spent a lot of time together. The solar rocket we've been designing for physics class is requiring a lot more work than we thought."

Sometimes humor can diffuse a rumor. "You think we're gay? Believe that and I'll sell you a chicken with lips!" If you're willing to bring the issue out in the open, others are more likely to relax around you.

At the same time, make extra efforts to live in a way that no one can criticize you. This may mean spending more time around other people. Instead of being alone with that one friend, invite a group over for a movie night. Or go bowling or play tennis in public where other people can see that you're doing nothing questionable. You won't have to do this forever. But it will help the rumor to die down. The internationally known evangelist Billy Graham has always been very conscious about his behavior. He's a married man, and throughout his career he refused to meet with any woman alone; he always insisted that a third person be present in the room. That way he avoided rumors about any sexual misconduct before they could start.

If people continue to whisper that you or your friend is gay, let others defend you. Maintaining close ties with several people instead of only one person means that there are several friends who know you well enough to speak up in your defense. My husband, Gene, is an ex-gay. He speaks on college campuses and in churches about how people with same-sex desires can change. One time a newspaper falsely reported that Gene told an audience that he'd had two gay encounters in the previous year. The reporter's error was serious enough to put Gene's job at risk. My husband didn't write to the newspaper, but our friends drafted letters that demanded an apology from the editor.

Our friends were confident in writing those letters because Gene's life is itself a testimony. Likewise, if every area of your life is consistently in line with what God commands, people will be more willing to believe you. When the newspaper report first came out, friends approached my husband and told him, "We knew you so well, we realized the story couldn't be true."

Rumors, however, do not die easily. Sometimes, despite every effort on your part, someone continues to talk. When that happens, you may have to take a step back and ask, *How important is it for this person, who spreads gossip, to respect me?* We all want people to like us, but that's not always possible. If you're a Christian, you may find that those who don't believe as you do will misinterpret your intentions.

At times, you may find that God himself is your only supporter. If that happens, you're not the first person to be in that position. For hundreds of years, people who obeyed God have been maligned. They've had to trust God to protect their reputations and defend them.

And that is what God did for my husband. God had already made a safety net: my husband's talk had been videotaped. After the news article first appeared, someone handed my husband a copy of the videotape. When the newspaper editor realized that his reporter had twisted the facts, the paper published corrections and extended an apology.

Whenever the truth is exposed, the person who started the rumor loses credibility. That person's own friends no longer trust him or her. As one man said, "They dug a pit for me and fell in it themselves" (Ps. 57:6, paraphrased).

Whom Can You Trust?

The fabric of friendship is held together by a thousand threads, but the strongest one is called *trust*. Rumors are like scissors that snip that thread. And when that happens, the whole piece unravels.

Nate trusted Jason; Kyle no longer did. Could the guys' friendship survive a rumor that they might be gay?

Chew on It

1. Had Nate and Jason done anything inappropriate? Why might people have thought they were gay?

2. What types of casual physical contact are acceptable for two girls who are friends? What is okay for two guys? How do these forms of contact differ?

3. Have you ever wondered if someone you saw in a crowd was gay? What made you think that person was gay? How well does your stereotype match reality?

4. How would you feel if people were talking about you and your friends? How would you deal with rumors?

5. The Bible says, "[Jesus] knew what people were really like. No one needed to tell him about human nature" (John 2:24–25). How does this statement relate to rumors?

5

What Do I Say . . . When I See Warning Signs?

KYLE SPEAKS

AFTER ALL YOU'VE HEARD about me from Nate and Jason, you must think I'm worse than the guys I arrest on the street. You may think I'm crazy. Maybe I am, but maybe I'm not. Let me tell you things from my perspective.

When Matthew Iron died, I felt great, knowing that one of my men had been the one to bring him down. The department always welcomes good publicity. But soon every newspaper reporter and TV journalist in the country showed up to interview Jason. I admit I got angry. Camera crews and men shoving microphones into my face mobbed the doors of our building. I had a job to do. When would things get back to normal? Trying to get my department in order was harder than getting a batch of snakes to march in a straight line.

Couldn't anyone keep some perspective? After all, I've been on plenty of dangerous assignments. Bullets have flown past my head. I've given my blood and sweat to this job for thirty years, most of them as commissioner. How many nights have I left my family at 3:00 AM to examine a homicide? Do talk show hosts ask to interview me?

Then my son and Jason became friends. Don't get me wrong. I liked Jason too . . . at first. But when Nate gave Jason his old high school varsity jacket, I can't describe what that did to me. For years I'd coached Nate in football. We spent hours outside tossing that ball. He was my son, but he was also my best friend. The year he made varsity, the team went to the finals. That jacket symbolized all we ever did together. The first time I saw Jason wearing Nate's jacket, something inside me snapped. Like Jason took something that belonged to Nate and me. I felt betrayed. Jason was taking my place in Nate's life. Yes, I lost my temper. Yes, I threw the guitar at Jason. And if I'd had a gun, I probably would have used it.

When rumors about the two guys being gay began to fly around the department, I knew they weren't true. But I didn't stop the rumors; I just looked the other way. Our department followed the army's lead: Don't ask, don't tell. But when Nate tried to talk to me and defend Jason, I used those rumors as a handy excuse.

I shouted, "You S.O.B.! If those rumors about you two guys being gay get into the news, you'll be toast! Even if the rumors don't go public, Jason's going to keep climbing and get my job someday. Don't you see what he's doing? When that happens, you'll be nothing!"

Nate never told you what I did next, did he? A land mine of anger exploded inside me. I keep my old army knife on my desk to open letters. I was so furious I threw that knife at my son. At my own son! Sure, I meant to kill him. I got even madder when the knife missed and bounced off the wall into the waste can.

Soon after that, Jason left the force. A couple dozen of my best men resigned at the same time.

New rumors began flying. People told me that Jason joined a street gang. Others said he was into hallucinogenic drugs. I knew that those rumors weren't true, either.

Finally someone saw Jason with some of Matthew Iron's men. That shocked me. Jason was an Eagle Scout, a God-and-country man. I couldn't accept the idea that he'd join a white supremacist group. At least now I had an excuse to go after him.

Nate was my second in command by this time. I couldn't depend on him to go out and arrest his best friend so I assigned a special unit to watch Jason's house. But Micki, my own daughter, helped him escape.

Who else could I turn to? I offered my men rewards—money, promotions, anything!—to bring him in. Didn't anyone else see that Jason was a threat?

Finally some tips trickled in. A migrant laborer gave a detailed account of seeing Jason at a soup kitchen. Then an elderly couple, assault victims, reported that a man matching Jason's description had chased their muggers away. At last, I thought, people are helping me. I never stopped to ask why they would turn on someone who had saved their lives.

I had no close friends of my own. My son? Nate still respected my authority but anyone could see he didn't trust me. My pastor? I'd thrown an occasional dollar in the offering plate at church but had never talked to the minister about anything more serious than the weather. How could I count on him for support? After what I'd done, surely even God was disgusted with me.

My computer became my salvation. I discovered an astrology Web site. I loved the anonymity. No one knew who I was. I poured out my problems, explained my fears. Someone out there must have looked at the moon and consulted the planets. The answer came back. "Everyone is a friend of the man who gives gifts. The poor man has no friends. They go far from you and though you pursue them, they are gone. You will die alone."

No! No! Even the stars were against me!

———

Nate's father was a lonely man. The two men he'd been closest to were Nate and Jason. They'd been loyal and continued to be loyal to him throughout this time. Jason, in all his media contacts, never once hinted to the press that the commissioner might be mentally unstable. Instead, Jason let the press think that he himself had cracked under pressure, that this was the reason he resigned.

Kyle drove away the very people who cared most about him. Instead of recognizing Nate and Jason as his friends, he perceived them as his enemies. Within three years, Kyle died. He and Nate were both killed in a freak encounter with another leader of Matthew Iron's group.

Kyle would have been shocked to see who became his replacement as head of the department: Jason became the new commissioner. What no one knew when Jason left the department was that he'd been asked to do some undercover work for a federal agency. His assignment? To infiltrate Iron's white supremacist movement. That assignment ended just days before Nate and Kyle died.

What went wrong with Kyle? What destroyed his friendship with the two men who admired him, and what kept him separated from the men who offered the emotional support he so desperately needed? Why was he so lonely?

Many gays, too, are lonely people. Family members freak out and leave them. Other friends exit when they hear the news. So far, I've suggested that abandoning a gay friend might not be the healthiest solution. But what are some warning signs that a friendship—any friendship, not just with a gay—is moving into dangerous territory?

Is It "Just Us"?

In the cartoon strip *Shoe*, the main character is a tough old bird. One day, he confesses to his associate, "You know, I'm friendlier than most people think. I do have a small circle of friends."

"Sure you do," his associate replies. "Zero is a small circle, isn't it?"

Long before Jason appeared on the scene, Kyle had problems making friends. Other than a counselor whom he saw occasionally, the only person close to him was his own son. Theirs was an exclusive relationship. When Jason became Nate's best friend, Kyle felt abandoned, betrayed. And jealous.

A key warning sign of an unhealthy friendship is a "just us" mentality. "You can't have any other friends—just me."

When I married, I moved to Pennsylvania where my husband taught college. The only person I knew on campus, other than my husband, was a single woman I'll call "Joan." Joan and I had been close friends years before, so when I arrived on campus, I eagerly sought her out to renew our friendship. I called Joan and suggested we go for a walk around campus. Her answer shocked me. "You're married now. We can't be friends anymore."

And our friendship ended. I later learned that Joan was a lesbian, but this could have happened in any heterosexual friendship. She couldn't face sharing our friendship with anyone else, not even my husband.

When a relationship becomes possessive, and your friend demands that you separate from other people, something is wrong.

Am I Free to Be Me?

One time when Jason was still on the force and visiting Nate's house, Jason didn't show up for dinner. Nate explained to his father that Jason had gone home to attend a birthday party for his younger sister. Kyle exploded in anger.

A friendship is sick when one person perceives any change in plans as a threat to the relationship. One person makes unreasonable demands of the other.

Suppose, for example, your friend spends all day focused on the time that you two can be together. This may involve fantasizing, obsessing about what the other person might be doing or thinking. The amount of time spent together becomes evidence that, "You really care about me." When you call to cancel an evening at the movies, no matter how reasonable your explanation, this friend thinks you don't care.

Maybe your friend lays a guilt trip on you for giving any other plan higher priority than his or her own. Perhaps this person insists you spend more time together the next day to prove you care. Something smells rotten in this friendship, and it isn't you.

Who Is in Charge?

Another warning sign appears when one person becomes consumed with making the other feel happy. Instead of demanding time and attention, someone uses you as an emotional barometer. If you're okay, your friend is okay. If you're sad, the friend feels responsible.

"Kendra" came from a broken home. She'd been abused emotionally and physically as a child. Everyone she ever trusted had let her down. When "Rhonda" came to work in the same office, the two girls hit it off. Soon they were having all-night movie sessions together on weekends. When Rhonda's husband complained, Rhonda snapped, "She needs me! I can't let her down like all those other people."

After several months, Rhonda left her husband and children so she could devote herself full-time to meeting Kendra's needs. The relationship with Kendra required all Rhonda's energy as she tried to demonstrate her unconditional love.

Who Is Benefiting?

Don't you hate to be used? One symptom of problems in a friendship might be when one friend attempts to "buy" friendship.

Kyle thought gifts of money or a promotion would motivate people to be his friends. He treated Jason that way. Like Jason was a yo-yo on a string. When Jason served a purpose, Kyle promoted him in the force and treated him like a member of the family. When Jason became too popular and threatened Kyle's position, the comissioner made up reasons to demote him. And Kyle used the same method on others. When Kyle wanted to capture Jason, he offered bonuses to his men.

There's a word for people like Kyle: manipulator. Manipulators turn out to be unreliable friends. You never know where you stand with them.

You remember Tom, who shared his story at the beginning of

this book? When Tom ran into problems with his friend Adam, Tom wondered if he himself was a manipulator. "Was I a master manipulator? I didn't even know what I was feeling until it was too late. Didn't Adam and Jessica know this was a time of discovery and awareness for me? Where was that understanding that I read about in the Christian books? What happened to forgiveness and reconciliation for people like me? What happened to the gospel? I felt lied to and manipulated as well!"

Tom felt that Jessica and Adam wanted him to change only so that it would enhance their own image as strong Christians. "I became a project to them. I learned that to be loved, I had to perform a certain way or live up to a certain standard. Being gay falls short. Having mixed and raw emotions falls short. Not knowing the answers to what to do with unwanted homosexual feelings falls short."

Are You Talking?

Nate tried to make his father understand how he was mistreating Jason. What happened? Instead of listening, Kyle raged.

"Heather" and her friend "Pam" had problems communicating. "I tried to discuss these communication problems with my boss, and while I was talking, Pam just butted in and cut me off mid-sentence. She blurted out, 'I totally disagree,' then went on about her feelings. That made me so upset. It didn't bother me that she disagreed with me and had another opinion, because that's healthy in friendships to have different opinions, to listen to each other to see another point of view. What upset me and made me even more ticked off was that she just cut me right off. It was as if what I had to say had no value. It made me feel like what I had to say was totally worthless. Like I was 'wrong' and what I said was not worthwhile, and I had nothing to contribute to the conversation."

Heather and Pam had other problems communicating. Pam, for instance, had a habit of not being on time. One evening she made Heather wait for her, and they ended up being late for a meeting at church. Heather says, "The entire drive there I was so frustrated, upset, and fed up with constantly having to apologize to everyone because 'we' were late. Plus the fact that, because of the prior events, I was definitely *not* in the mood, *not* in the right frame of mind, and *not* wanting to 'worship the Lord.' Needless to say, it was very difficult for me not to show everything that was going on inside of me."

The problem here not only involved Pam's being late. Heather couldn't communicate her feelings. When friends can't talk or won't listen, a friendship may be on shaky ground.

Is It Physical?

Up until now, every warning sign we've discussed about friendships could apply to gays or heterosexuals. What about when behavior starts to get intimate?

A quick hug upon greeting or leaving a same-sex friend is normal. Even guys can hug. I'm serious! But what happens when the hug lingers? What happens when a kiss is exchanged? What if the kiss moves from a cheek to the lips?

This is one area where male-male and female-female friendships differ. In our world, society allows women greater degrees of physical intimacy than it allows men. Such allowances, though, instead of making life simpler for women, make it harder. A woman can slide into a lesbian relationship more easily than a man can slip unintentionally into a gay one.

In the case of Rhonda and Kendra, Rhonda put her arm around Kendra to comfort her after Kendra's family rejected her. When they watched a video, it seemed natural for the girls to snuggle on the couch. Since Rhonda's husband rarely displayed affection, these times met Rhonda's needs as much as Kendra's. One night the girls fell asleep in that position.

When Rhonda left her husband and moved to Kendra's place, the girls were around each other every evening. Still, Rhonda fooled herself into thinking that she was helping Kendra, giving her a security she'd never known. And soon the girls shared a bed.

When did the girls step across a line? It all seemed like a smooth continuum. They had slipped into a lesbian relationship, though Rhonda had never thought of herself as gay.

Because women, like Rhonda, are naturally compassionate, they can slide unawares across boundaries of intimacy. Women need to be careful, to step back and evaluate their female friendships from time to time. How does one particular friendship compare with others that you know are healthy? Does the level of physical intimacy in this friendship exceed that in your other friendships? Would you stay at this level of affection if other people were present in the room?

For men, the steps into physical intimacy are different. Body contact doesn't slowly move from a sideways hug to a facing hug to a passionate embrace. Instead, the shift toward a physical relationship is more intentional. Marcus invites Tico to attend a sporting event several hours from home. When the event is over and it's late, Marcos suggests they "spend the night" at a hotel, opening the door to a homosexual encounter.

Men hardly ever wander unknowingly into a gay relationship. If behavior is getting physical between two guys, they're already in the danger zone.

What's Important Now?

Here's one more caution sign that indicates an unhealthy friendship: priorities turn upside down. Things that were important a year ago fade in magnitude.

"Don" had a wife. He was a soccer dad. He stood on the sidelines and cheered every time his kids played a game. He served as a leader in his church. Then "Jared" walked into his life.

Don's wife began noticing changes. Her husband opened a separate savings account. He dyed his hair to get rid of the gray. He set up a new post office box. He began smoking again, after four years without a cigarette. Then one day Don removed his wedding ring.

Within a year, none of the things that were at the top of Don's list mattered anymore. He felt Jared was more important than his wife. Don walked out of his marriage, never showed up at his kids' games, and left the church. Everything about him screamed, "I'm different now. Leave me alone."

His family pointed out the changes, but Don refused to listen to those who cared for him most, just as Kyle tuned out Nate and Jason.

What About You?

Perhaps, as you've read this chapter, you've recognized a pattern of unhealthy friendships in your own life. You may not be gay, but are you like Kyle, demanding the exclusive attention of your friend? Have you tried to control your friend's activities? This may be a signal for you to seek help.

To whom could you turn? Look at the people around you. Who models healthy friendships? A grandparent? A neighbor? A teacher? If you attend a church, your pastor may be a place to start. Even if you aren't part of a congregation, many pastors are willing to listen to someone who wants to talk.

Requesting help can be pretty intimidating. An easy way to begin is to approach someone you've selected and invite that person to go for a walk. Outside—away from phones, noisy televisions, and younger kids who run into the room—you'll discover conversations begin naturally. You could ask, "Who's your best friend? How did you meet? What's most valuable to you in a friend?" As you begin to relax, bring up some of the questions you are wrestling with. "How do you think I should handle this? How can I avoid manipulating my friends in the future?"

If the person you're talking to isn't certain how to help you, ask that person to suggest someone who might be able to help. He or she may recommend a professional counselor. Scary as that may sound, some wise counsel now could save you years of pain later.

Should I Leave?

What if you're in Jason's position? You've been hurt by someone like Kyle, a person who's important in your life. Many people who are wounded don't stick around to work through the issues. When a friendship goes sour, they go out and get new friends. Those same people often carry that same attitude over into marriage. As long as things go okay, they stay married. When things get rough, they divorce.

Before you discard your friend or a spouse, take stock of the situation. What is your motive for abandoning ship?

Suppose the friendship has become physical. Maybe your friend is gay. Do you feel that if you hang around your friend, you won't be able to resist the invitation to physical intimacy? What if your friend were doing drugs? Do you feel you might start shooting up if you continue to associate with this person? *If you're tempted, get out of there!* The Bible tells Christians to fight for the truth but to flee temptation (1 Cor. 6:18; 1 Tim. 6:11; 2 Tim. 2:22). But do your friend a favor before you leave: explain the reason you're bailing. Don't leave friends guessing, imagining the worst about themselves.

On the other hand, what if your only motive for leaving is "people say my friend is gay" or "I feel uncomfortable." Breaking contact may be the wrong step for several reasons.

First, cutting the cords of a friendship may be harder than you think. If this person goes to the same school as you, are you prepared to switch schools? If you both work for the same company, will you change jobs? If your friend attends the same church, would you leave for a different church? What if this individual lives next door? Will you move to a new home?

Second, perhaps your relationship with this person is only the most recent in a long string of unhealthy relationships your friend has had. One more break may leave this person unable to cope. If you leave, the individual may question his or her value as a person. Has anyone ever been honest enough with your friend to point out to him or her why previous friendships have failed? You may help most by encouraging your friend to seek professional counseling before the pattern occurs again.

Third, if you're a Christian, you'll have to ignore all the places in the New Testament that command us to live in peace with one another (e.g., Phil. 2:1–2). Christ's last prayer in the Garden was that those who followed him would live in unity (John 17:22–23). If we run away from our Christian friend when a problem arises, how can we look Christ in the face?

Jesus said healthy people don't need a doctor. He came to help the ones in pain (Mark 2:17). He didn't discard friends who made his life difficult. From the moment he chose Judas as a disciple, Jesus knew that Judas wasn't the type of person most of us would want as a friend (John 6:70–71). Judas wanted to use Jesus for his own purposes; he urged Jesus to begin a revolution in order to kick the Roman army out of the country. A manipulator, that's what Judas was. He was also a thief. He stole money from the group's petty cash (John 12:4–6). He couldn't be trusted. Not a good foundation for a friendship.

But did Jesus shove Judas to one side? For three years Jesus allowed Judas to walk next to the other disciples, to hear all the stories and to see all the miracles. When at the betrayal Judas revealed the true nature of his personality, his actions only highlighted the incredible extent of Christ's patience and love.

Shouldn't we show the same respect to our friends? Can we expect a free ride through life when Jesus had to deal with this type of person? Never forget that the person you're dealing with—gay or straight—is of infinite value to God.

What If I Stick Around?

If you decide to stay, what can you do to repair the situation?

Communicate! Tell your friend how you feel, but be careful as you pick your words. True, Jesus was pretty blunt when he told Peter to back off. He told Peter, "Get away from me, Satan" (Mark

8:33). Not exactly tactful, but by the time this happened, Jesus and Peter had such a strong trust level established that Peter accepted the rebuke and didn't go off in a huff. And Peter's hide was tough as a rhino's.

You, on the other hand, may have to be more gentle. Saying "I feel like a prisoner when I'm around you" might be the equivalent of erecting a barbed wire fence between you and your friend. But try words like, "I feel uncomfortable when you . . ." or, "I feel pressured when you . . ."

Maybe you need to ask forgiveness. Did you talk behind your friend's back? Have you made fun of this person in a crowd?

And let your friend know why you've decided to stay in the picture: you value the friendship.

Go Ahead and Commit!

Remember the image of a plaster cast? A decision to work things out can hold you and your friend together while your friendship heals like a broken bone. In the case of Jason and Nate, Kyle refused to wear that cast. He rejected each opportunity to restore his friendship with Jason, then he pushed his own son away. Kyle died without recognizing the two best friends he had.

Chew on It

1. Why did Jason choose to resign from the force? How did this demonstrate that Kyle could have trusted him? Would you have done the same thing?

2. What emotions kept Kyle from recognizing Jason was his friend? Have you ever felt these emotions? When?

3. Name three people you trust. Why do you trust them? Would those reasons change if they were gay?

4. What would cause someone who was gay to trust *you*?

5. A man in the Bible said, "Even my best friend, the one I trusted completely, the one who shared my food, has turned against me" (Ps. 41:9). How would you feel if you trusted someone who then used you and double-crossed you? What would that person have to do to regain your trust?

6

What Do I Say . . . When Courts Affirm Gay Marriage Is Okay?

MICKI SPEAKS

WAS JASON GAY? When I heard the rumors, I was shocked. For heaven's sake, I was engaged to the guy! I needed to know for sure, especially since his supposed "partner" was my own brother!

I'd seen Jason on TV long before Dad brought him home for the first time, so when I finally met him face-to-face, I acted cool, like it was nothing to meet somebody famous. After all, to him, I was the boss's daughter.

All the girls on campus talked like crazy about Jason. My brother Nathan laughed when I told him I was in love. Brothers can be a royal pain, but you should have seen Nathan's face a year or so later when Jason announced that we planned to marry!

And those rumors about Jason being gay? I won't lie. The rumors hurt. It took a lot of trust to go through with the engagement. But now that we've been married over ten years, don't you think I'd know by now? Still the rumors seem to have a life of their own. Every few years, people drag the issue out and dust it off to see if there's anything to it. I say, give it a rest!

Sure, Jason wasn't perfect. He had a few rough edges. He'd lived most of his life in the country. When we first dated, I was amused when he didn't open the car door for me and didn't know which fork to use at a formal dinner. Little things like that kept coming up. I know this sounds stupid, but when you're eating at the country club with the mayor or a local congressman, these things say a lot about a person. Jason really appreciated any help I could give him, and he learned fast.

A few years after we married, and later when Jason became the new commissioner, those rough edges grated on me. Things that seemed cute at first irritated me later. Like the dancing. It was one thing when we danced at the club. Jason would hold me close. I loved having his strong arms around me, every woman in the room wishing she were in my place. Then he went to the Ethnic Arts Festival.

Every year, local nonprofits sponsor a big festival at the civic center. Lots of celebrities attend. Jason was watching a group from the Polish Catholic church perform when one of the women invited him to join their line dance. Jason laughed, stripped off his shirt like the other men, and began to imitate their steps.

Some women worry about their husbands coming home with liquor on their breath. Mine comes home reeking of kielbasa and sauerkraut!

And the photos! The local TV channel camera zeroed in on Jason hugging this round lady in a greasy apron.

"Jason!" I told him at breakfast, "What were you thinking? I mean, what will I say to the mayor's wife and the members of the women's club when they see that clip? Didn't you realize reporters had cameras there?"

He laughed and reached for the newspaper. Then I lost control. I grabbed his arm and said, "Jason, listen to me. When we married, Dad gave us the BMW. He paid for this house. He introduced you to all the key people at the chamber of congress. You owe it to him to keep up the family image.

"For that matter, think about all I've done for you. After you quit your job and Dad sent men looking to arrest you, who got you out of the house just in time to save your skin? Don't you care how I feel when you mix with these ethnic types?"

When I finished talking, Jason stared at me as if I'd slapped his face. I couldn't believe what he said next.

"Michelle," he said—and right there I knew he was upset because he always called me Micki—"Michelle, that's enough! You know I love you. You know I worked hard for your father. I respected him even after he turned against me. If you're so worried about appearances, why didn't you worry long ago when your father had a mental breakdown? How did that episode affect the family's reputation? Oh, I accepted his gift of this house. Yes, I attended your big fancy church with its smells and bells! But if you think I'm going to stop mixing with ordinary people on the street now that I'm the new commissioner, think again. You say I'm embarrassing the family. You tell me your father gave me everything we have. No! You're wrong. God gave me this job. He gave me this responsibility and, whether you believe it or not, he gave me you. If I have to choose between some fancy reputation and God, God's going to win every time."

And then Jason walked out of the room. I knew he meant what he said. You remember that my father had a terrible temper? His anger destroyed him. Well, that day with Jason, I discovered I had the same kind of temper, and it almost destroyed our marriage.

Micki was right. Her marriage took a nosedive. Jason respected her space, but he played his guitar more and kept to himself. You see, Jason had loved Micki's father. He died. Jason loved her brother Nate. He died, too. And Jason loved Micki. When she hurt him, it felt like another death in the family.

Jason didn't divorce Micki. He still loved her, but he poured his energy into caring for Nate's son, Seth. Jason had promised to look after Nate's family if anything ever happened to his friend, and he kept that promise. Right after Michelle's explosion of anger, Jason began remodeling the basement so Seth could move in.

Marriage can be pretty tough. Like friendship, it can start off okay, but sooner or later you hit stony ground, as Jason and Michelle did. One person embarrasses the other, perhaps unintentionally. Communication falters. Hurts accumulate. Jason and Micki were able to talk about their feelings, but many marriages end in divorce.

When you think about all that can go wrong between a husband and a wife, why do so many gays fight for the right to marry? For that matter, why would *anyone* want to enter this kind of relationship?

What's the Big Deal About Marriage?

A long time ago, God said it was not good for man to live alone. The Lord could have given Adam a friend named John. Instead, he gave Adam a wife named Eve. In our society, gays may acknowledge that the first marriage was a guy and a girl, but they ask, "Does that mean that all marriages have to follow that pattern?" Many courts today are saying no.

For a full answer to this question, we need to understand the institution called marriage and what God intended it to represent. Once we know that, we can see if a relationship between two people who are gay fits God's expectations of marriage.

First, marriage is different from other relationships—like friendships—that we've already discussed. Sure, we get to pick our friends and we get to pick our marriage partner, but a lot more is going on in marriage: marriage should be based on a friendship, but not all friendships lead to marriage.

Friendships are the training ground for marriage.

The wedding ceremony unites two people who grew up in different families. After the honeymoon, each person must adjust to the other person's habits. This process can create stress and test each person's commitment to the other. My husband says, "Marriage was full of surprises. Fortunately for me, all of them were good ones." If one partner is unwilling to change, the relationship can become strained or even rip apart. When bitterness festers, when trust is broken, or when the person you love leaves for someone else, a marriage may collapse. The person who has never learned how to resolve problems of anger or distrust in a friendship may not have the expertise or commitment to handle conflict with a spouse.

Remember those former roommates my husband and I had at college? The ones that patiently rubbed off different rough edges of our personalities? The result? When Gene and I finally married, the transition was a smooth one. So smooth, in fact, that some of our friends kidded us about being "old-lyweds."

People who haven't learned to form strong friendships are not yet ready for marriage. That's because the best marriages are built on a foundation of friendship.

Marriage Involves Physical Intimacy

When I first asked people how friendship and marriage differed, people gave me the most obvious answer: marriage involves sexual intimacy. Friendship doesn't. Friends don't usually share the same bed. Golfing buddies don't sleep together, members of the book club don't climb under the sheets with one another.

Marriage is the green light for sex! Did you know that God's very first command in the Garden of Eden was to tell Adam to have sex with his wife? God said, "Be fruitful and multiply," or in other words, "Go for it!" Has it ever occurred to you that the sexual organs are the only parts of the body that require the participation of another person to fulfill their natural purpose? The male and female parts fit together comfortably and pleasurably. A husband and wife enjoy a level of intimacy on a physical level that enhances their intimacy on every other level.

What happens when two guys or two girls seek physical intimacy in a gay relationship? If you'll permit me to be blunt, the parts just don't fit. Substituting alternative body parts can result in serious damage to organs that were designed for other functions.

Think back to when you were a kid. Did your mother ever tell you not to jump on the furniture? Maybe she was worried that you'd hurt yourself. One day when my daughter was two years old, she was jumping on my bed. I warned her to stop before she fell, but sure enough, a minute later she slipped and cracked her collarbone. Or maybe your mother worried more about the furniture than you. She may have said something like, "Don't use the couch as a trampoline! No one designed it for that. You'll break it!" Another example? If you borrow your father's car and use it as a battering ram, it might serve that purpose a time or two, but sooner or later someone (you) or something (the car) may get hurt.

If you use something in a way that violates its original design, something or someone can get hurt. Using an exit as an entrance is not a smart idea. When God said sex is for a man and a woman, a male and a female in a relationship called marriage, maybe he had a reason to say that. Even when a court of law says sodomy is okay, it can't change the reality of how the human body was designed.

It's Not Just About Sex

But there's more to marriage than having sex. Marriage is like legal cement.

Lots of people who aren't married have sex. They think they're getting something wonderful; they enjoy the physical intimacy of sex, but then they discover something is missing. Instead of having a marriage built on a solid concrete foundation, they discover the cement never set. Now their feet are stuck in muck.

The guy who has sex with his gay partner may talk about love, but will he be there after the sun comes up the next morning? The girl in bed with her lesbian lover may enjoy the physical intimacy, but how will she feel when that person walks out?

Marriage is more than a promise whispered in an ear under the sheets of passion. A marriage is sealed by a formal covenant. It is a *public commitment*. For months, you plan a wedding. You invite family and friends to the ceremony. You make promises in front of the whole crowd. And did it ever occur to you that, during the public ceremony, everyone there knows what you will be doing in private that night on the honeymoon? And imagine this: Mom and Dad not only know you'll have sex, they even hope you'll enjoy it!

Marriage is more than a public statement of intention. It is a formal, permanent seal on a relationship between a man and a woman, a *legal contract* that carries the full weight of the law. If one person wakes up on Tuesday and says, "I don't feel married anymore," that person's feelings don't change the reality of the legal promise. Removing a ring from your finger doesn't make the marriage disappear.

"Wait," you say. "Jason promised Nate that he'd look after Nate's family. Wasn't that like a marriage vow?" No, it wasn't the same. First, Jason made a private promise, not a public commitment in a formal ceremony in front of all their friends. Second, it was not legally binding in the eyes of the law. Third, it was no wedding vow. At the time they made the promise, each of the guys already had a wife.

So why can't gays make that public commitment? Why do Christians get uptight and claim that allowing gays to marry would threaten the institution of marriage? Maybe the physical parts don't fit, but gays can see themselves making this type of promise.

It's a Lifetime Together

Have you ever stood on the sidelines and watched a couple break up after they'd dated for a long time? When Jeremy Duncan in the popular cartoon strip called *Zits* breaks up with his girlfriend, Sarah, he's feeling blue. His friend Hector sits next to him and tries to cheer him up but feels awkward offering a hug. He says, "If you weren't a guy, I'd give you a hug." Jeremy replies, "Thanks. If you weren't a guy, I'd take it." Breakups are painful.

A college student, Lauren, was talking with other teens about dating and marriage. Lauren emphasized the need for commitment. One girl nodded her head and remarked, "My boyfriend and I have been together for *two years*!"

Lauren grinned, "Honey, I'm not talking about *two* years. I'm talking *fifty* years!"

Friends may spend hours together, but when two people marry they embark on a lifetime together. Marriage is an exclusive relationship, and each person's primary commitment is to his or her spouse. Friends come second.

Friendships tend to ebb and flow like ocean tides. My husband has a good friend named Curt. They think alike, maxing out on philosophical issues one day, matching wits another. They both enjoy science fiction. Though Curt lives two hundred feet away, Curt and Gene hardly ever see each other. Each works full-time. When Curt stops by to drop off a book, however, the conversation that follows may last for hours. If Gene crosses the street to help Curt overcome a computer glitch, I may not see my husband until it's time for supper. Then weeks, even months, may pass before the two guys talk again.

Ebb and flow. Lapses and surges in contact. Some of my friends have moved out of state. I see them once a year or even less often.

Marriage is a constant. A man and his wife live together. When one picks up and moves to another state, the other is expected to go along. If husband and wife are separated for a time while the house sells, the intent is to be together. That responsibility to each other comes before commitments to friends.

Marriage requires the soldering of goals and priorities into one strong unit. My husband and I had to work through that merger. Before we got engaged, I had plans to enter a university in Mexico and get my doctoral degree. Gene supported my goal of doing graduate work, but neither of us wanted to be separated for three to five years after the wedding as I traveled thousands of miles away to pursue my studies. No way! We agreed that I'd look for graduate programs closer to our home. My husband and I also wanted to start a family. Having kids means another long-term commitment.

Again, though, gays can see themselves in this type of relationship. They want the security of a lifelong commitment. Indeed, some gay relationships last far longer than heterosexual marriages.

Gays want to have families, too, by adopting kids and raising them. Once again, gays ask, "Is it fair to say that we can't marry?"

It Makes "Cents" to Merge!

Two, three, or even four people can be close friends, but each person maintains his or her unique goals and separate identity. Marriage, on the other hand, creates a whole new entity.

When several people get together and form a business corporation, in the eyes of the law they're no longer separate individuals. Their business is a new economic unit that never existed before. When a male and female vow to marry "for richer, for poorer," that promise reflects that they, too, are now a new economic unit that never existed before.

Gays argue in court that married couples have all the financial advantages. The IRS grants tax benefits to married couples. Spouses have visitation privileges at hospitals and in jails. Insurance companies extend health benefits to spouses. Employers give time off for bereavement, and they pay survivor benefits to the remaining spouse. Courts recognize the rights to child custody or alimony when two people have been married.

People who demand rights to gay marriage want the same financial and legal benefits that a husband and wife share. We need pretty strong reasons to deny gay couples these benefits.

It's Holding Each Other Accountable

A good friend holds another friend accountable. When I see old friends after months or years apart, I might ask them what God has been doing in their lives. The same thing happens in marriage but at a higher intensity. The physical and spiritual realities of each spouse is constantly evident to the other.

When I'm with a friend, I can hide some of the unsavory aspects of my personality. We're not around each other twenty-four hours a day, seven days a week. I can avoid talking to someone by not returning a phone call. I could pretend that I deleted his or her e-mail message. But when two people marry, every morning they wake up and face their spouse. When I first married, I'd try to wake up before Gene, climb out of bed, and quickly brush my hair before he opened his eyes. That didn't last long. We agreed that the stubble on his face was no more or less appealing than my own disheveled hair. Your spouse is going to see you at your less-than-dazzling best.

Just as you see each other's physical realities, you begin to see the inside of your husband or wife. That person becomes part of your own soul. When we lie in bed together, I can tell when Gene's thoughts are churning over issues he faces at work.

Before my husband and I were married, Gene told me about his struggle with homosexuality. Those intimate encounters with other men were like acid that burned a hole in his memory. Just because he married, those memories did not disappear. He still faced homosexual temptation. Early in our marriage, Gene and I talked about it and agreed that from time to time I should ask him point-blank, "How are you dealing with temptation?" I didn't badger him, bringing it up over and over, but once or twice a year I *did* ask. Today, Gene knows that at any time in the future I might ask. And knowing I might ask helps him resist temptation.

I always feel awkward bringing up the question, but I care about Gene. This is something he wants me to do. It's important to our marriage so, no matter how hard it is, I make myself ask.

That is a very intimate level of accountability. And once more, gays feel that they have a right to that type of relationship in marriage. Thus, other than the physical parts not fitting, we have not yet found a strong argument against gay marriage.

It Involves Authority and Submission

I might not make friends by writing these next paragraphs, but marriage involves authority and submission. There's got to be one person who takes responsibility. According to the Bible, that person is the husband.

In a friendship, each person is on equal footing. This might not be true if your friend also happens to be your boss, but generally one friend is not responsible for the other person.

Marriage is different. The Bible describes the man as the head of the woman, just like the brain of a body is in control of the rest of the body (Eph. 5:23–30). Don't get me wrong. This picture is one of protection, not power. The brain sends out signals to the hand to warn it to move away from a hot flame. The ears hear the sound of an intruder in the house, and the brain sends adrenalin to the nerves to prepare for flight. Just because the man is the head, though, doesn't mean that a husband can abuse or ignore his wife. The man is responsible for the woman. It is his job to be sure she is cared for and protected.

I watch my friend Jim look after his wife, Melinda, who suffers from multiple sclerosis. His patience overwhelms me. Day after day he helps her dress. He prepares meals. He tenderly lifts her to her bed. He designs unique devices to make her life more bearable. He protects her.

At another place in the Bible, it says that the person who believes in God must obey those in authority because those authorities are responsible for that person's soul (Heb. 13:17). Again, don't leap to conclusions. I'm not saying that a woman is saved through her husband's faith. All I mean is that Scripture holds the husband accountable for nurturing her soul. God authorized the husband to look after the woman. When that man and woman stand before God at the end of time, God will ask the husband for a report of how he cared for the woman. Ouch. The buck stops here. How any man has the guts to take on that kind of responsibility for another person's soul is beyond my understanding. If men were like me, they'd all chicken out of marriage and the human race would die out!

And the wife? Is she just a doormat placidly lying there without any say in decisions? No, a loving husband listens. The husband wants to do what is best for her. The husband loves her. Any woman who wants to marry a man should ask herself, *Is this a person I could*

submit to? Am I confident that he has my best interests in mind? Does
he respect me?

When the woman puts the wedding ring on her finger, she is
joining a team. Her husband is the captain, but he can't succeed
without the cooperation of the team. She does everything in her
power to help him, including following his lead. They both work
hard to move toward the same goal. If success comes, the whole
team wins, not just the captain, because they worked together to
achieve a goal.

This picture of authority and submission does not apply to two
people of the same sex who want to marry. Which one will God
hold responsible for the other's soul? The authority roles become
confused, and Scripture states clearly that God is not the author of
confusion (1 Cor. 14:33).

What About the Right to Privacy?

Some may ask, "What gives some religious fanatic the right to tell
gays what they can or can't do in the privacy of their own bedrooms?
For that matter, what right does a judge have to sit in front of a court-
room and tell people what they can or can't do in their own homes?"

Every citizen born in the United States has certain basic
rights that are guaranteed in the U.S. Constitution. Though the
Constitution never mentions a right to privacy, let's suppose that
there were such a right.

If someone willfully disregards a law, the authorities can arrest
that person whether the act was done in public or private. Let's say
a student pirates music from the Web in the privacy of his own
home. It's still against the law. The student can claim that everyone
does it, that it doesn't hurt anyone, that it was done in the privacy
of his own home, but the fact remains that he's disregarded the laws
that were established by his government. Privacy is no defense.

Laws in our country establish that marriage is between a male
and female. So change the laws about marriage, right? Just change
the definition of marriage, okay? In a democracy, voters can always

work to change the rules, but the blunt truth is that God's kingdom is not a democracy. His rules do not change. And he sees what goes on behind closed doors.

One Male and One Female

The strongest argument for traditional marriages being between one man and one woman is not simply that the body parts fit together. The strongest argument is that this is the way God planned it: marriage is for one male and one female.

Way back in the time of Genesis, God established a pattern of marriage between one male (Adam) and one female (Eve). He affirmed that pattern for two thousand years. Jesus reaffirmed it in the Sermon on the Mount.

Today people want to change the pattern God established. They try to go behind the fence and play the game with different rules. What happens when we ignore the rules of a game? Suppose the coach of a baseball team decides he wants to put extra players in the outfield. Will people protest? If we install basketball hoops on a baseball diamond, is it still the same game? What will the umpire say? God made the rules for marriage, and we have to play by his rules.

Some people don't like the way God wrote his laws, but experience has shown me that every time I follow God's plan, things go better. God says, for example, that I shouldn't tell lies. When I obey and choose to tell the truth, I discover my life is less complicated. Lying might seem simple at first. It might even seem kinder than telling the truth. But deception always results in problems. God is wise and his rules for life make sense.

Many young people today think they can ignore God's command to wait for sex until marriage. After all, they reason, if sex is pleasurable, why would God give us something so wonderful and then not let us enjoy it? In my office, I see people who have chosen to ignore God's rules. I watched "Amber" deal with the aftermath of having sex before she was married. She discovered the pain of broken relationships, the stress of raising first one child and then two alone, and the embarrassment of dealing with a sexually trans-mitted disease. Following God's plan about waiting for sex until marriage didn't make sense to Amber when she was young—but now it does. God set his rules in place to protect young people like Amber from getting hurt. His desire was not to turn our world into a prison but to protect us so that we could enjoy sex to the fullest in the right context—a context called marriage.

We may not understand why God made certain rules, we may not always like them, but we can trust that God knows what he is doing and has good reasons for it. Those are the rules, and whether we like them or not, God's laws still have authority over our lives.

Why Is God Against Gay Marriage?

Why can't God just accept the fact that some people are gay and leave them alone? Can't they have a civil union and live a quiet life, being faithful to their same-sex partner?

When God created human beings, he made them in his image. A male by himself did not reflect all of God's nature. A female by herself could not reveal all of God's personality. So he made those first humans male and female, not male and male. Each reflected different aspects of God's character. A male/male or female/female relationship fails to reflect the complete picture of God's person. The image would be as distorted as a reflection in a curved fun-house mirror.

In a book called Song of Songs,[1] God describes the physical at-traction of a groom for his bride and the bride for her husband. Words like "sweet," "pleasing," "enchanting," "delightful," and "perfect" portray the physical attraction of a man for his wife. There is no parallel passage in the Bible that glorifies a sexual at-traction of one male for another male. On the contrary, passages that describe sexual relationships between people of the same sex use words like "unnatural" and "shameful" (Rom. 1:26–27). It is not the person God rejects but the unnatural relationship. It's not the way he designed things to work.

God used the intimacy between a husband and wife as a picture of his own relationship with the church (Eph. 5:23–24). The commitment between a male and a female in marriage represented God's commitment to the church. God never draws a similar analogy that involves a same-sex relationship.

Sounds Like Lots of Cold Showers Ahead!

Where does this leave your friend who is gay? No marriage? No sex? Thanks a lot! Sounds like a pretty miserable life, eh? If a gay person can't marry, how does he or she satisfy that yearning for a lifelong relationship involving intimacy and commitment? What if your friend wants a family?

God understands the yearning of every person for these things and he longs to fill that need. He offers each person, straight or gay, a chance to enter into an intimate relationship with Christ. God has already made a commitment "for better or for worse" and "for richer, for poorer." He has promised to stand with each of his children not just "until death us do part" but for all eternity! He offers to adopt each of us into his forever family. Now that's good news worth sharing with any friend, straight or gay!

Intimacy with God sounds good on paper, but sometimes people want to hug someone with skin. Once when my daughter was a little girl, she asked me if God had arms. I told her that God didn't have a body like ours. "Then how does he hug?" she asked. I pulled her close to me in my arms and replied, "When he needs to give you a hug, he reaches down and borrows my arms." When a person wants to obey God in the area of sexual self-control and has need for a hug, God uses good friends like you to fill the gap.

Is it really possible to be celibate and happy? To be honest? Yes! Look around for some positive role models. And hang on, because there's more good news coming in the next chapters.

Nate died just before Jason's marriage to Micki hit rocky soil. That's when Jason turned to God for support no earthly friend could provide.

Chew on It

1. What do you think Jason learned in his friendship with Nate that became important in his marriage? How would having a good friend before marriage help you to become a better partner in marriage?

2. Review the qualities of a friend listed in chapter 3. What additional qualities would you like to have in the person you marry?

3. What would you say to a gay friend who wanted to marry his or her lover?

4. How could you respond appropriately to your gay friend's need for affection?

5. A man in the Bible was grieving over the death of his best friend. He said, "[His] love . . . was . . . deeper than the love of women" (2 Sam. 1:26). What do you think he meant? (Hint: note the plural form, *women*.)

7

What Do I Say . . . When People Claim God Hates Gays?

JASON SPEAKS

WHEN NATE AND HIS father died, my world crumbled around me. To lose—in one night—both of these people who had made such a difference in my life seemed more than I could bear.

"God!" I cried, "How could you let this happen? I can understand Kyle's dying. He couldn't have kept his job much longer. Most people, even Nate, recognized that he wasn't the man they once knew. He was getting older, emotionally unstable. Still, God, why did you have to take Nate as well? Wasn't it enough to take his father? You knew Nate and I weren't gay. Couldn't you have left my best friend behind?"

Nate gave me more support than most wives give their husbands. He had always prayed for me. When he died and those prayers stopped, I could feel the difference. I felt vulnerable, as if someone had ripped off my bulletproof vest. I felt . . . alone.

I asked myself, *Does God make mistakes? Does he really understand how much I hurt? Is he as just as everyone says he is?*

Then God spoke. "Don't look anxiously about you for help. No friend is ever going to be able to help you the way I can. When you were on the team in high school, you and your buddies would pump each other up, saying, 'We can do it! We can win!' or, 'Great play! Awesome!' But nobody remembers that game today. Jason, don't look to others for encouragement. Look to me. I'm the one who helped you then. I'm the one who can help you now" (Isa. 41:6–10, paraphrased).

———

Jason's questions were natural ones. Jason hurt. We all want support and encouragement when we struggle with pain. Just as others do, gays ask, "God, do you care when I hurt?" Gays need the assurance that God is powerful, that he can be trusted.

As a friend, you want to be there for your gay friend, but you can help a person only so far. You have a life of your own—family, school, job, other priorities. You can't solve all your own problems, let alone those that plague your friend. There comes a time when all of us need a friend who's bigger than life. Someone who can be there any time, any place you have a problem. That ultimate friend has a name. He's God.

At the beginning of this book, my friend Tom related how he came out to Adam and Jessica about his secret struggle with homosexual desires. Tom was a Christian. He trusted God, and because of that he thought he could trust his Christian friends, too. When they broke that trust, they destroyed a friendship, but they also shattered Tom's confidence in God. It's taken years to rebuild the basics of his faith.

Only God is perfectly reliable. Only God can put up with you even when you can't stand yourself. Only God trusts you when you aren't ready to trust yourself. Only God, who has the wisdom of thousands of years, can help you and your friends make right choices for the future.

Doesn't God Hate Gays?

In the *For Better or For Worse* cartoon strip, when Mike learns that his friend Lawrence was kicked out of his home because he was gay, Mike goes looking for Lawrence. He finds him staring at a cup of coffee in a nearby cafe. Mike says how sorry he is that Lawrence's family kicked him out. Defensive, Lawrence responds, "Yeah? Well, I'm not the first gay to be thrown out onto the street and I won't be the last. And I don't need anyone to feel sorry for me, okay?" Mike sits down across the table from his friend and replies, "Fine . . . is it okay if I feel angry for you?"

If Mike felt bad for his gay friend who was hurting, how much more do you think God grieves when he sees someone struggling with same-sex desires?

Perhaps you've heard that God hates gays. One young man battled his same-sex desires alone for months and finally mustered the courage to ask his pastor for help. That pastor looked him in the eye and told him, "There's nothing I can do for you. You're already damned. God hates gays." If this were true, would you seek God's help if you were gay?

Fortunately that young man turned to my husband for counsel. Gene introduced him to a God who doesn't spurn the person who's in pain but reaches out to heal and restore. This is a God who says, "You are precious to me. You are honored, and I love you" (Isa. 43:4).

In chapter 2 we saw how Jesus cared for the leper, the prostitute, the widow, the orphan, the tax collector. These people, whom everyone else wanted to marginalize, were the ones Jesus reached out to. He went into their homes. He ate meals with them. He loved them.

Far from abandoning gays, God desires to be their friend. He yearns to bring healing and hope into their lives.

Does God Make People Gay?

Perhaps your gay friend says, "If God makes people and I was born gay, then he's responsible and I'm off the hook."

Some people who are gay claim that they were born that way. If it's natural, just part of one's DNA, why fight it? The truth is, to date, no such "gay" gene has been found. In fact, many people in the gay community do not want homosexuality to be a genetic trait. They feel that if chromosomes predetermine whether a person has blue eyes and curly hair or if the genes decide before birth whether a person is gay, then being gay can't also be a choice. Such people, who promote gay relationships as just another option for any person to choose, want to downplay any biological studies that suggest a gay gene.

Other gays feel trapped in a body that doesn't seem to fit. Did God play some kind of vast cosmic joke on these people by giving them desires that don't match their bodies? Was God satisfying some sadistic sense of humor? Does he sit up there in heaven laughing as gay people struggle to fit gender roles that belong to other people?

God takes responsibility for the way he makes each one of us. A man named Moses claimed that he didn't have to obey God because he had a handicap. When God told him to lead Israel out of Egypt, he told God, "I'm clumsy with words. I'm no speaker." But God refused to accept that excuse. God demanded, "Who makes mouths? . . . Who makes people so they can speak or not speak, hear or not hear, see or not see? Is it not I, the LORD?" (Exod. 4:11). God knew that Moses' real weakness was fear. Moses was worried about his own skin; after all, a murder charge was still hanging over his head if he returned to Egypt.

Another man, Jeremiah, claimed he was too young to obey God (Jer. 1:6–8). Did Jeremiah think God's timing was off, that God had put him in the womb of his mother a few years too late? "It's your fault, God." God refused to accept that as a defense. The root issue? Jeremiah feared that God couldn't be trusted to get him through the difficulties that lay ahead.

Those who believe they are born gay might want to talk to someone born with a physical challenge. Such a person asks many of the same questions. Why was I born deaf? What did I do to deserve this wheelchair?

Back in the times when Jesus lived on earth, people thought any physical abnormality or mental problem resulted from a person disobeying God. That's why, when Jesus and some of his followers saw a man born blind, they asked Jesus, "Who sinned, this man or his parents?" (John 9:2 NIV).

Bzzzt. Wrong question. None of the above. Jesus replied, "Neither. He was born blind so that the power of God could be seen in him."

Why are some people gay? The roots often lie buried deep in the private graves of their own lives. You and I may never be privileged to know why a friend is gay, but I do know that when a person turns to Jesus Christ, God uses that opportunity to display his strength in the person's life. God can give that person power to live according to God's plan. The result? God is honored!

When he walked on earth, Jesus showed us how to depend on God's power for every need. Refusing to draw on his divine privileges, he leaned on God to resist all sexual desires—heterosexual or homosexual. Among those who followed Jesus, there were a variety of women, including prostitutes, who knew all too well how to entice a man (Luke 7:37–39; 8:1–3). Jesus spent large amounts of time in close association with twelve men. His consistent and appropriate behavior in his relationships with both males and females demonstrate that it is possible to live a life of purity no matter what sexual desires a person may have.

If God didn't have the power to support a person walking away from homosexuality, or if God had the power and refused to share it with that person, God might be accused of being unfair. But God does have the power, and he will pass that power on to all who call on him for help.

Does God Make Mistakes?

Perhaps your gay friend doesn't have a gay chromosome but you know that he or she had a bad experience as a child. People who have homosexual desires often blame someone else for their desires. They might blame an alcoholic parent, the absent father, or the domineering mother. Or the neighbor who inappropriately touched the gay person when he or she was a child. Gays may want to blame God. It's his fault. Where was God when these things happened?

Does God goof up occasionally? Was he out grabbing a doughnut when your friend was sexually abused by a neighbor? Then God came back in and said, "Whoops! Look what happened while I took my coffee break!"

If God makes mistakes—even one mistake—then God is not God. He is not perfect. He is not powerful enough to help you get through a math exam, let alone cope with cancer, the death of a parent, or whatever crisis you face. He is not that megafriend you need.

But the truth is, God *is* perfect. He doesn't mess up when he makes people. People are the ones who goof up. Scripture says that every individual is born with a flaw (Ps. 51:5). Theologians call that flaw a sin nature. Every one of us enters the world with a desire to ignore God and go our own way.

Any weaknesses in our bodies or minds can cause us to turn to God for help or turn away in anger. Some of us have visible disadvantages like a shortened leg. Others of us have less tangible ones such as a temper or unwanted sexual desires. Any of these situations can lead to rebellion against God. The person in a wheelchair can curse God or choose to lean on him for help. An individual who has a temper can let it loose on his boss or ask God for power to respond with gentle words. And those who have unwanted sexual cravings can give in to those desires or they can ask God to supply strength to control those feelings.

The question is not "Did God make a mistake?" but "Will I trust God to meet my unique needs?"

Who Gets Hurt If I Am Gay?

What's the problem if two gays love each other and decide to live together? If the Bible says "God is love," and if God is good, then how can loving someone be wrong?

The simple answer is not that loving is wrong, but love can be expressed in inappropriate ways. Sexual intimacy—any form of physical intimacy—outside marriage is like powerful glue. When you bond sexually with another person, it's like you're glued to that person. When you break up and move apart, it feels like your gut is being ripped in two. Who gets hurt? Each person who was sexually intimate.

All the pain that occurs when a guy-girl relationship breaks up is just as likely to happen when a same-sex relationship splits up. "Bill" moved in with a gay man he met at work. Then that man left him for another lover. Bill became so depressed he couldn't work for a month. His doctor put him on heavy doses of antidepressants. Another man named "Paul" talked about suicide when his male lover left him. Paul felt the depression of being rejected as deeply as any heterosexual male would feel when his girl walks off with another guy.

Far more than emotional pain results if a person acts on his or her desire for a gay relationship. The choice to disobey God in one area of a person's life gradually infects other areas of his or her life.

Before "Bob" married "Linda," he mentioned that, in the past, he'd been attracted to other men. After the wedding, Bob spent a great deal of time hanging around a gay friend, but still Bob insisted to his wife that he wasn't sexually intimate with this other man. Then Bob went on a business trip to the West Coast. He told Linda he'd be traveling by himself, but she later learned that the gay friend went along. She felt betrayed. Some time later, Linda came home and found Bob weeping in their living room. He cowered in terror, saying that the police would be coming to arrest him: he'd been making obscene phone calls. Then, when working on family accounts, Linda was shocked to learn that Bob had run up enormous credit card bills buying clothes to impress his lover. Bob had always prided himself on handling money carefully.

Did Bob's relationship with his friend stop at sexual attraction? No, his choice about sex influenced other areas of his life, causing him to do things that contradicted his basic values: lying to his wife, making obscene phone calls, and ruining the family finances.

When a person engages in same-sex sexual intimacy, who else gets hurt? The future spouse. When one relationship breaks up, the next relationship is also affected. Memories of sexual intimacy hang around. When another person comes along, comparisons are made. Jealousy, anger, and hurt from the first relationship intrude on the second, undermining the new relationship from the very beginning.

Other people who are associated with a gay person may feel pain, too. Time and again, I've seen the people on the sidelines of gay relationships get hurt. While Bob lived daily with the fear of going to jail as a result of his actions, his wife, Linda, wept at his betrayal, and the people who received the obscene phone calls were also affected. When a gay person leaves his or her family for a same-sex lover, the spouse and children suffer the consequences of that person's choice to abandon all that he or she once considered important. The brother of a lesbian stresses out wondering if she will contract an STD. The parents of an HIV-positive gay grieve as they stand by his grave.

God grieves, too. When a gay person decides that being with a lover is more important than a relationship with God, that person often leaves the church. When a gay walks away from God, he or she has delivered a slap in the face to the most faithful Friend of all.

Is Being Gay the "Unforgivable Sin"?

A young man who struggles with same-sex attractions tells me he understands that being gay is not the worst sin in God's eyes.

Still, this young man senses that people in the church view him as, in his words, "uniquely perverted."

God's first concern is not whether a person is attracted to males or females but whether that person is attracted to HIM! Physical purity is important, but spiritual purity is essential.

The "unforgivable sin" involves a vigorous rejection of God's Spirit of Truth (see Matt. 12:31–32; Mark 3:28–29; Luke 12:10). Like a witness under oath in a court of law, the Holy Spirit tells us the truth. He testifies that Jesus offers a gift of forgiveness and salvation to both gays and straights, but some people reject that truth and turn away. When a person refuses to trust Christ, he or she says, "The Spirit is lying. My problem is so big that not even you, God, can handle it. Not even Jesus' death on the cross is enough to pay for my sin." That attitude is not forgivable. Why? Because that person is rejecting the only medicine that could heal his or her pain—Jesus Christ.

Pride can keep a person from leaning on God. By refusing to trust God, a person who is gay cuts off the only power strong enough to forgive him or her for any past acts and to transform that person into wholeness. But when a person turns to Christ, that person can tap into ample power to meet any need and into hope to face the future.

Why Can't We "Pray It Away"?

So if a person trusts Christ, all storm clouds on the horizon will fade and the sun will shine forever—right? Many people living with the problem of unwanted same-sex attraction think that God should take away those desires as soon as a person becomes a Christian. After all, the gay person has prayed and asked God to remove the desire, and God answers prayer, right? Why doesn't he wave his celestial wand and turn gays into straights as soon as they're baptized?

The answer is the same one Jesus gave to the people in his hometown. He told them that there were many widows in the time of Elijah, but God sent the prophet to help just one widow in a small town called Zarephath (Luke 4:24–26). Certainly God has the power to do miracles, and he could change all gays into straights, but often he chooses to work through other methods. The miracle may not be in removing an unwanted desire. The real miracle is the testimony of the person who daily turns to God for strength to resist continuing temptation. Those unwanted desires may be the very things that cause this person to seek God over and over. Because I desire to eat all day, every day, many pages of my prayer journal are full of pleas to God for strength to resist the cookies, crackers, and chips that call out to me from buffet tables and grocery store shelves. If God took away my desire for food, I know I might be thinner, but my prayer journal would be thinner too! Why would God take away the very thing that causes me to seek him?

"Jesse" prayed for years that God would take away his desire for other men, but instead of disappearing, those feelings continued to torment him. And when he went to see a counselor, the problem got worse because Jesse had to recall the time his own father molested him. As he recalled details of that event, he remembered that two other men also molested him as a child. Then, when members of his family learned of his struggle, Jesse felt exposed. Angry at God for not answering his prayers to take away this same-sex attraction, Jesse chose to abandon both his family and his faith for a gay lover.

Jesse never realized that all along God was indeed answering his prayers. God wanted to heal him but knew Jesse needed to understand the original causes of his pain. God also wanted Jesse's family to be part of the solution, becoming part of a support network embracing this young man. Far from turning a deaf ear to Jesse's prayers, God was hard at work, but Jesse didn't recognize the way God answered his request.

If someone claims to be a Christian and continues to struggle with same-sex desires, it doesn't necessarily mean that person is not saved. Don't confuse temptation to sin with giving in to sin. Jesus faced temptation every day while here on earth (Heb. 4:15).

You can be sure that Satan tried to tempt him with pride each time Jesus performed a miracle, but Jesus refused to give in.

We may not be certain whether a gay friend is really a Christian. Only God knows for sure what is in the heart of a man (John 2:24–25). Your part is to be there on the sidelines, praying and encouraging your friend to reach up for God's help.

What If I'm Gay? Is There Hope?

Suppose you've been reading this whole book and a small doubt has been gnawing at the back of your brain. Perhaps you're wondering if *you* might be gay. What should you do? Is it already too late to change?

First, it is never too late. If you're uncertain whether or not you are gay, or if you're considering trying out a homosexual relationship, don't test the waters. Sexual intimacy—any sexual intimacy, gay or straight, outside the bonds of marriage—creates powerful memories that can impact a future relationship with a spouse.

Do you remember, back when you were in second grade, how the girls lined up on one side of the room and boys on the other? In those days the boys were afraid of "girl cooties." As you grew older, did you discover that your classmates' attitudes changed? By middle school, some of the guys were looking at the girls in a new light. A person's feelings toward the opposite sex ten years ago may not be the same today. Though you may not feel attracted to the opposite sex at this point in life, your feelings are not cast in concrete. You may find that your feelings will shift in the future. You don't want to do something now that might spoil your enjoyment of a sexual relationship in marriage ten or fifteen years from now.

If you've already been sexually intimate with another person of the same sex, stop. The fact that you did something in the past doesn't mean you have to continue doing it in the future. Did you ever steal some coins from your mom's purse when you were a kid? Does that mean you have to grow up to be a professional thief? What you did in the past is in the past. If you ask God to forgive you, the death of his Son on the cross can take care of that. We're talking about choices you will make in the future.

Stopping is not easy. You'll need help, so the next step is to seek counsel. Asking someone for help is not a sign of weakness. It takes guts to say you want to change. When I first married, I knew my husband wanted children but I wasn't interested in having kids. I decided to talk to a counselor. Over time I developed a new perspective. The responsibility of raising a child still scared me. I felt unsure I had what it took to be a mother, but my counselor encouraged me to step up to the challenge. Today I'm grateful for three wonderful children. Help from a good counselor can make an enormous difference in your life.

It's important, though, to find the right counselor. Many counselors, including some Christian counselors, feel that homosexuality is nothing to worry about. They accept it as just another choice. These counselors want you to accept yourself the way you are and not try to change. They say gay is okay. Yet these counselors work hard to help other people facing different circumstances to make better choices. If a father or mother were beating a small child, the counselor wouldn't say that beating a child is just another choice; the counselor would help that parent learn the skills necessary to control a violent temper. If somebody in deep depression comes to a counselor, he or she wouldn't tell the depressed person to accept the situation as it is or to consider suicide; the counselor would offer help. When you want to find a counselor, look for someone who'll help you learn to say no to inappropriate sexual desires.

Exodus International is an ex-gay ministry, offering help to those who face same-sex attraction. The organization offers books, tapes, videos, and conferences, but it especially offers support groups and individual counseling for gays who want to become obedient to God in the area of sexual purity. Too often a young person feels alone, as Tom did at the start of this book. "I'm the only one I know who feels this way." Exodus offers a safe place to meet others who have been gay and who also want to follow Jesus' leading into a new way of life.

If there is not an Exodus support group in your local area, their e-mail list offers a way to contact people who will offer support and information on better choices for your future. In the meantime, you can also look around your church for same-sex role models who can teach you what it means to be a Christian guy or a woman of God. My husband, Gene, grew up without a strong male role model. After his father left the family, Gene became involved with other men in homosexual behavior. When Gene headed off to college, he began attending a church in his college town. He met a family at that church who seemed to have everything his own family lacked in warmth and love, so he made an intentional effort to get to know this family. Like an FBI agent, Gene "spied" on the father, mother, and kids to learn how the males and females interacted, and then he adopted many of those patterns as his own. Today, as his wife, I benefit from what Gene learned.

Whether you find help from a counselor, from Exodus, or from a healthy role model in your own backyard, a day will come when you will no longer define your identity by your same-sex attraction but by your relationship with Christ.

Why Would God Want Me as a Friend?

Some people act as if it's okay to treat gays badly: *Everyone will understand if I make fun of that person.* But once more, imagine you were the one with homosexual desires. Who would want to be your friend? Why would God want to be your friend?

Abraham, a man who lived thousands of years ago, learned to lean on God over and over again. He was called the "friend of God" (2 Chron. 20:7; Isa. 41:8). When Abraham was an old man, God wanted to give his friend a gift. Abraham said, "God, what good are any more gifts? I have plenty of money and servants. What I really desire is a son" (Gen. 15:2, paraphrased). Abraham's arms ached to hold a child next to his heart. God answered that request and gave Abraham a son named Isaac.

God, too, has all he needs. Money? Poof! He can make as much as he wants. Servants? He has thousands of angels waiting on him hand and foot. What he really wants is a relationship with us. The truth is, God offers us much more than friendship. He offers adoption. He wants to adopt us as his children (John 1:12). Like Abraham, God wants children he can hold next to his heart.

Your heavenly Father is waiting for you to come with your pain, whether it involves sexual issues or not, and turn to him for help. Jason had a father who barely noticed him. When he met Nate's dad, Jason felt he finally had a real father. Then, after Kyle rejected him, Jason turned in grief to God and discovered that his Megafriend was actually his Forever-Father.

For Further Information

Web Site

See www.exodus-international.org.

Books

Brestin, Dee. *The Friendships of Women.* Wheaton: Victor Books, 1988.

Davies, Bob, and Lori Rentzel. *Coming Out of Homosexuality: New Freedom for Men and Women.* Downers Grove, IL: InterVarsity Press, 1992.

Konrad, Kyle. *You Don't Have to Be Gay.* Hilo, HI: Pacific Publishing, 1987.

Morrill, Cathy. *Soulutions: Relational Healing for the Next Generation.* Santa Monica, CA: Desert Stream Press, 2000.

Thompson, Chad W. *Loving Homosexuals as Jesus Would: A Fresh Christian Approach.* Grand Rapids: Brazos Press, 2004.

Worthen, Anita, and Bob Davies. *Someone I Love Is Gay: How Family and Friends Can Respond.* Downers Grove, IL: InterVarsity Press, 1996.

Chew on It

1. Why do you think God allowed Nate to die at the same time as his father?

2. How would you answer someone who told you God hates gays?

3. What "handicaps" in *your* life keep you from trusting God?

4. Who would be hurt in your world if you became sexually active before marriage?

5. Jesus welcomed people rejected by their society. What do the following statements tell you about God's love for those who trust him?

    Those the Father has given me will come to me, and I will never reject them. (John 6:37)

    No one will snatch them away from me, for my Father has given them to me, and he is more powerful than anyone else. So no one can take them from me. (John 10:28–29)

8

What Do I Say...
When I Want to Help?

JASON SPEAKS

THE WAY I MOURNED after Nate's death, you probably think I had only one friend, or maybe you figure that Nate and I really were gay. It's true that we had a unique friendship, and when he died, I felt like my world ripped in two. But I'd never have made it through that experience, or lots of others since that time, without the support of additional friends.

Sure, I had my wife to help me, but there comes a time when only another guy understands what you're going through. Hank, Barry, Shawn, and Mac were the ones who rallied around and held me together, not only when Nate died but when I hit another bad spot a few years later.

Again, rumors caused the problem. A big lawsuit put my job on the line.

That's when it pays to have good friends. Hank was the first one at my door to encourage me. He didn't care if people saw him with me in public, no matter how many cameras flashed. Because he still worked in the same department, he promised to be my inside man and keep me up-to-date on the latest developments.

Until things settled down, the department suspended me. Without pay! Then they froze my assets, too, so I couldn't touch my savings. How's a person supposed to feed his family and pay the mortgage if there's no money coming in?

This time Barry, Shawn, and Mac came to my side. They offered a lot more than a Hallmark card. Shawn isn't rich. He has a family of his own, but he showed up with a wheelbarrow full of produce from his garden . . . fresh tomatoes, green beans, corn. His wife sent along homemade bread. Mac handed me a gift certificate to the grocery store. And Barry? He paid my mortgage!

Finally everything settled down. The judge threw out the lawsuit, and I got my job back, but there's no way I can ever repay the kind of support my friends provided. When I tried to return the money Barry had given me, he told me flat out to forget it. You could have picked me up off the floor. Over a thousand dollars? Who could ever forget that kind of friend?

———

J ason had good friends who helped him through rough times. We all need people who come alongside us and lift us up when we can't face life on our own. We've seen that people who are gay are no different. They need good friends who know how to help, when to stay quiet, when to speak.

Not all friendships are the same. Some are superficial, but others reach into the core of your soul like Jason's friendships with Nate, Hank, and the other guys.

My husband, Gene, teaches with a dozen colleagues in the math department at his college. Though he sees these people every day and enjoys a working relationship with them, he rarely encounters Wayne outside the context of campus unless they happen to attend a professional conference together.

Gene and Paul, another co-worker, challenge each other in a variety of arenas. Over a lunch together, they talk about computers but might just as easily discuss personal philosophies.

Then there's Bob. Gene's friendship with Bob has moved beyond exchanging thoughts. When a concern weighs on Gene's heart—

when he's stressed out and needs someone to pray with—Bob's the man.

Though all these men teach math and computers for a living, and Gene might label any of them his friend, the level of intimacy in these friendships is very different. Given the similar social context, you might think they'd all relate to each other in the same way, but they don't. Nor is it as simple as the number of years spent together. Gene has known both Wayne and Bob for over twenty-five years, but he's able to share a deeper level of himself with Bob.

What Are Levels of Friendship?

First, there are people with whom you share activities. You get together and watch a movie, shoot hoops, or chow down on hot dogs. This group can be small or large. You know them casually and enjoy being around them, but the commitment level is low. Some friends in this category may, in fact, be gay but you'll never know it because that issue never comes up.

Next is a smaller circle of friends that you bond with on another level. You're on the same wavelength . . . brain waves, that is. Conversation moves beyond events on a calendar to thoughts in your head. It's not quite a Vulcan "mind meld" but getting closer. Again, you might not know if one of these people is gay. You might discuss the political or psychological aspects of homosexuality but you might never learn that the person you were talking to struggled with same-sex attraction.

Finally, there's a select group of friends with whom you enjoy that deeper level of emotional and spiritual intimacy. With these people you feel safe sharing felt needs, hurts. One of these friends might say, "My father told me last night he plans to leave Mom." Or, "I was counting on getting that scholarship. Now I don't know if I can go to college." Or . . . , "I'm gay."

This select group includes the kind of friends on whom Jason leaned when his world fell apart. If a person you know within such a small circle tells you he or she is gay, be careful. So much is invested in the friendship that both you and your friend feel vulnerable. If you walk out of the picture, your friend may feel like a marathon runner who collapses with the finish line in sight.

Not all Jason's friends stood by him when he faced trouble. Phil, one of his good friends, turned his back on him. Jason said, "It wasn't an enemy that made fun of me—I could have handled that. It wasn't an opponent who insulted me—I could have walked away from him. But it was my partner, my buddy, my close friend. He pretended to be concerned and visited me when I was sick, but all he did was gather information to start rumors."

When a friendship collapses, how do you help your friend to stand up again and move forward?

Broaden the Horizons!

When "Dean" left his wife, "Barbara," to live with his gay lover, Barbara needed friends to help her put her life back together. The first time she talked with me, Barbara couldn't bring herself to say the word *homosexual*. She felt like a failure as a woman. If her husband had left her for another woman, she might have felt she could change something about herself to make herself more attractive to her husband. She could lose weight or clean the house better or cook tastier meals. But how could she become a male? Barbara needed other women who could gather around her and tell her she still had worth. Her friends performed CPR on her soul.

Gays, too, need a circle of friends, not just one friend. If a person confides in you about his or her struggle with gender identity, make sure you're not the only one this person leans on. If you are, you may feel trapped and responsible to "solve the problem." When I'm helping a person—straight or gay—I encourage the person to develop a small network of people they can turn to. That way, if I can't be reached, then the person has other friends who can help.

If someone claims that you're the only friend he or she has, help that person develop new friendships by drawing him or her into the larger circle of your acquaintances, a pool of people with whom you share activities. "Mike," after battling same-sex attrac-tions for years, felt alone when he came to my husband for help. Gene and I took him to our church. In a class there, Mike met several people who became the support network he craved. Later, when he was deeply depressed and needed help, we were out of town on vacation, but another friend in the class filled Mike's need for support.

Maybe your gay friend already has a circle of close friends. These people are also gay. Should you tell your friend to stop associating with these people? No. This group is your friend's current support network. Letting go of these friends with only the vague hope of making new ones is scary. Insistence that your friend leave his or her gay buddies could have a negative effect: Your friend may de-cide it's easier to drop one person, *you*, than lose a whole circle of gay friends. And—who knows?—someone else may be praying for those other people. If you reject your friend's associates, you may offend the very person someone else is striving to help.

What's Gay? What's Okay?

People who teach courses on alcohol abuse often encourage stu-dents to try on a special pair of glasses. The lenses distort the vision much as a few mugs of beer would impair a driver. The student wearing the glasses discovers how hard it is to discern a straight line. Depth perception is off and the student stumbles through an obstacle course.

Many people who face same-sex attractions come from emotion-ally unhealthy homes. Their perception of gender roles becomes distorted as they struggle to see through a filter of pain.

Perhaps the lesbian's father never affirmed his daughter. He never told her that he loved her or was proud of her. Instead, he may have abused her or her mother physically, emotionally, or sexually. As a result, the daughter may now see all females as weak persons, and she may reject the idea of becoming a doormat herself. If she perceives females as somehow having less value than males, she may adopt masculine roles to avoid further abuse. She may step into the role of protector for another female.

The homosexual male, on the other hand, may have rejected his father as a positive role model. He hasn't a clue how a man acts as a father or husband. My husband came from a broken home. His mother spent many of his childhood years in a mental hospital. Gene perceived women as weak and unstable. His father stuck around until Gene was old enough to get a driver's license and then handed him the keys to the car. Then his dad left town . . . for good. Having no clear role model for either father or mother, Gene turned to other men for the affection lacking in his home.

If someone you know is gay, you can fill an important function, helping your friend to recognize healthy gender roles. "Denise" finds her lesbian desires confuse her when she attempts to relate to other young women in appropriate ways. In her mind, she constantly replays her conversations with young women she knows: *Did I say the right thing? Could it have been misinterpreted as a come-on? Should I call her, explain that I'm gay and apologize for what I said? Or should I just let it pass and hope she took it the right way?*

Her thoughts become a tangled web, exhausting Denise as she fights against a multitude of threads. While this battle is occupying her mind, Denise can't focus on her work. Hours go by as her mind churns over her questions. Then she looks at the clock and realizes it's close to quitting time. She hasn't accomplished her tasks at her desk. Now a new fear attacks Denise: She wonders if she'll lose her job!

How can she break this cycle that threatens to overwhelm her? One thing Denise does is call me. When the cycle begins, she picks up the phone and dials my number. "Emily, I said this . . . was that okay?"

I can assure her that I might have said the same thing to one of my girlfriends: "Yes, it was appropriate. No, it probably wasn't perceived as a come-on." After my assurance and a brief prayer, Denise begins to relax and get back to work. Slowly she's learning what healthy same-sex friendships look like.

When your gay friends display appropriate male or female roles, affirm them. Be specific. Encouragement that simply says, "good job!" doesn't tell your friend what action resulted in that remark. Try something like, "I appreciated your help when you took on responsibility for editing the newsletter. People really look to you for leadership." Keep it sincere. We all can spot a phony!

What More Can I Do?

Remember the tendency to hang a neon sign that says "gay" around your friend's neck? That sign distorts your perception and keeps you from seeing other dimensions of this person. Are *you* focused on sexual desires every waking moment of *your* day? Neither is your friend. Gays have many dimensions to their personalities that you may not notice if you always scrutinize them through a "gay" filter.

Go back to the chapter called "What Do I Say ... When Friends Tell Me They Are Gay?" and review some of the qualities of a healthy friendship—respect, for example, or confidentiality and trust. Note again how few of them have anything to do with sexual orientation. As you get to know gays, affirm their positive qualities. Many gays are especially thoughtful, can communicate well, and are sensitive to the needs of people around them.

Another thing you can do is allow your friend to talk. Don't jump in with answers. Listen. When you do talk, remember that even if you don't have same-sex desires, you have areas where you're weak. It might relieve your gay friend to know that straights also fight sexual desires or to realize that you, too, face temptation, though it might be in a different area, like overeating.

Be prepared for confusion. When a person is working through such an emotionally charged issue, the feelings come tumbling out in random order, like clothes tossed about in a drier. The feelings may be contradictory. There may be joy at no longer being isolated, anger at those who contributed to the original pain, insecurity about further rejection. The relief of no longer holding the secret alone can cause a person to release emotions that have nothing to do with his or her sexual orientation. It's as if every emotion in the heart must be taken out, shaken about, and reexamined, a process that stirs up a lot of dust.

Recognize real limitations for yourself. You can't control a gay friend's sexual choices or actions any more than you can control what your friend decides to eat for dinner. If you try to turn your friend into a rehab project, you'll end up frustrated. Besides, how would you like someone to constantly be on your case to change?

Settle in for the long haul. Issues of gender identity aren't solved in an hour while talking over a cold Coke. If your friend has rejected his or her gender role for years, it probably will take years to rethink that identity. In the meantime, hang in there.

Respect confidentiality. If someone your friend counted on in the past abused that trust, your friend may be fearful of relying on you. When someone confides in you that he or she is gay, don't destroy the fragile trust your friend has placed in you by talking to others without permission.

Set clear boundaries for your friend. Your friend should not monopolize your time or your energy or your thoughts. Remind your friend that you are not a professional counselor. When the crowd followed Jesus to the house of a man named Jairus, Jesus told them, "Nobody comes in except Peter, James, and John" (Mark 5:37, paraphrased). It's okay to set boundaries. If someone calls my husband on the phone and he has to be somewhere in fifteen minutes, he says clearly, "You can have ten minutes of my time." If the person rambles, Gene reminds them of the limit again after five minutes. When the time is up, he says good-bye. Setting clear boundaries helps the caller to use the time wisely.

What else can you do? Must you just sit idly by on the sidelines? No. Take action by learning more about same-sex attraction. Prepare for the questions your friend will soon ask. The list at the end of chapter 7 offers some resources that will help you. By reading one or more of the books listed, you'll be able to answer the questions when they come, or be able to point your friend toward people who have answers.

Christians, though, can do a lot more. Ask God to work in your friend's life. Let your friend know that you want to pray for him or her . . . in *any* area of life, not just in the area of sexual attraction. God may reach your friend first in another area of his or her life and deal later with the issue of sexual identity. My friend Tom says, "I ache for the love of Christ and his gospel to be taken to the gay community. I want them to know, to truly feel and believe that no matter what, God loves them and died for them. They don't have to change their orientation before God will love them and save them. They don't have to change anything about themselves to earn love, or perform to get his approval. But before this message can be carried to the gay community and be in any way convincing, Christians must learn it themselves."

Ever have trouble remembering to pray for a friend? Here's a hint: Think of an area in your own life where you struggle to obey God. Each time you stumble across that area of temptation, turn the temptation into a reminder to pray for your gay friend. If, for example, you're tempted to overeat, tape a photo of your gay friend on the refrigerator door. When you reach into the fridge for that midnight snack, try substituting a prayer on behalf of your friend. You might end up praying more—or eating less. Either way you win!

What if My Friend Doesn't Want to Change?

What if your friend isn't interested in changing his or her sexual orientation? What if he or she asks, "What's wrong with being gay?" You can still take all the steps to help that are mentioned above, whether your friend is interested in change or not. You can offer friendship, foster a safe environment for communication, be trustworthy, learn about gay issues, and pray on your own—all without any effort at all on your friend's part.

And don't assume that all change must occur at your friend's end. You may not be struggling with gay issues, but your friend might find one or two (or more!) areas in your own life where you're not living up to God's standards. Allow your friend to teach you, too.

Should you tell your gay friend, "What you're doing is wrong"? He or she already realizes that this is not the way God designed sex. The person who is gay has worked hard to suppress this thought. As with nuts and bolts, the male goes inside the female. A house built using only nuts or only bolts won't stand strong. God's laws make sense, and people who ignore those laws discover there are natural consequences. Can we overlook, for example, the studies that show the average life span of a sexually active gay is less than fifty years when the average heterosexual lives over seventy years?

You, as the friend, don't have to put on a black robe and preach about sin or threaten damnation. God's Spirit is able to speak inside the heart of a person. It's the Holy Spirit's job to point out things that need correction in our lives, and he does an excellent job of that without your help!

One important caution for young women helping males facing homosexual issues: The male/female dynamic creates problems of its own. The girl must be on guard against romantic expectations from the friendship. What begins with the best of intentions can cloud over when the girl feels needed by the guy and interprets that feeling as romantic interest. She can also become manipulative or try to be his "savior." Beware! When the guy does not meet her new expectations of a dating relationship, she will feel crushed.

Will I Become Gay? Is It Contagious?

Same-sex attraction is not contagious like the flu. You can't catch it just by being around someone who's gay. You can even have physical contact. Contact sports, backslapping, a brief hug are all appropriate.

There's a *Jump Start* cartoon in which the main character Joe is reading a book on male bonding. He's surprised when the book says it is okay for him to give his dad a bear hug. Joe says, "The handshake squeezed between the bodies only applies to buddies and distant cousins! Yikes! It's okay for you to kiss me too!" Putting an arm around his son's shoulder, the father replies, "Who wrote this book? It's great!" His son says, "The author is too embarrassed to reveal his identity."

Many gays feel rejected, like lepers in ancient times. Jesus shocked people around him when he reached out his hand and made contact with the skin of a leper, the eyes of a man born blind, or the corpse of a child. Others in the crowd were afraid of becoming contaminated, but Jesus knew how important a touch can be in the healing process. Your willingness to touch a gay friend says, "I'm not afraid of you." Someone once told me that our culture is oversexed because it is undertouched.

Some types of touches are not appropriate. You might not consider a hand to the face, for example, or an arm around the waist to be intrusive, but would you feel that way if your waitress at the burger shop caressed your hair while taking your order? These touches step into our personal space. A girl who's been sexually abused is especially sensitive to physical contact. The best approach? Ask permission before reaching out to touch someone, unless it's by phone!

Maintain your other friendships while developing the friendship with your gay buddy. Those other friendships are like a thermometer for checking the temperature of your relationship with the gay person. Do other friends call you six times each week? Are they upset if you change plans? If others are aware of your friend's same-sex attraction, ask them to give you an honest appraisal of how you're doing in balancing your desire to accept the gay friend and your desire to stand firm in your own beliefs.

Don't forget to maintain your own relationship with God. He will help you find that balance and give you wisdom to handle this friendship.

Jason wasn't gay, but when his world fell apart, his friends helped hold him together. More importantly, his main support came from God.

Chew on It

1. Jason had other friends when Nate died. Who would com-
    fort you if you lost your best friend?

2. Name one person in your own life who might fit into each of
    the following levels of friendship:
    *   acquaintance (shared activities)
    *   associate (shared thoughts)
    *   soul mate (shared needs)

3. If you can't think of anyone who fits your idea of a soul
    mate, what is it that keeps you from deepening your friend-
    ships with some of your associates?

4. Look around your home. Where would be a good place to
    hang a reminder to pray for a friend who is gay?

5. "There are 'friends' who destroy each other, but a real friend
    sticks closer than a brother" (Prov. 18:24). What does this
    statement tell you about helping your friends?

9

What Do I Say . . . When My Friend Needs Hope?

Do you swear to tell the truth, the whole truth, and nothing but the truth, so help you God?"

The truth is that neither "Jason" nor "Nate" was ever a police officer, but they *were* real people. Now the time has arrived to reveal their true identities.

Jason's real name was David, and he lived over three thousand years ago. His story is found in the Bible. As the youngest of a brood of boys, David developed a tough skin. His father, Jesse, had a pretty low opinion of this son. When, for example, a priest named Samuel asked to meet Jesse's sons, Jesse introduced all his older sons, but he didn't even think to call David in from the fields where he was working (1 Sam. 16:11). There were his sons, and, oh yes, there was David. David, the afterthought. The father's attitude infected David's brothers; his brothers bossed him about too (1 Sam. 17:28).

Tables turned when David went up against the leader of an army from a country called Philistia. Back in those days, the Philistines had the corner on the market for making iron, and their man was covered from head to toe in iron. "Matthew Iron," you see, was Goliath. Goliath was full of himself. And David, alone, with no

state-of-the-art weapons, killed this giant of a man (1 Sam. 17).
Suddenly David, the insignificant kid brother, became David, the
newest national hero.

"Nate" was really named Jonathan. Leading an uphill battle at
odds of ten to one against him, he routed an entire army (1 Sam. 14).
Similar experiences in battle cemented a deep friendship between
him and David. As the oldest son of the king, Jonathan was the
crown prince of Israel, but he accepted the fact that he would never
sit on the throne. That honor would go to his best friend, David.

"Kyle" was King Saul, the first king of the Jews. Saul had a problem with anger. Early in his life, his temper wasn't obvious. People
sneered at his authority when he became king, but he remained silent (1 Sam. 10:27). He even went so far as to defend those who had
mocked him (1 Sam. 11:12–13). But Saul became impatient (1 Sam.
10:8; 13:5–12). He unleashed his anger, in turn, at those closest to
him. Saul's love for David turned to hate when the younger man
became more popular than Saul himself (1 Sam. 18:7–8). Saul
raged when his daughter helped David escape (1 Sam. 19:11–17).
Saul threw a spear at his own son when Jonathan stood up for his
friend (1 Sam. 20:30–33). Saul's sometime therapist was actually
a priest named Samuel, and after Samuel died, Saul consulted not
an astrology site on the Web but a witch (1 Sam. 28:7–25). The re-
markable fact was that when King Saul died, David grieved and
mourned this ruler's death (2 Sam. 1:19–27).

And "Micki"? Her real name was Michal. She wasn't all bad. As
you know, she helped David get away from Saul. But her admira-
tion for David faded when he took off his shirt, bared his chest,
and danced in front of the women of the town. Humiliated, she
needled David about being indecent (2 Sam. 6:16–23). David never
divorced her, but right after this incident, he turned his attention to
caring for Jonathan's son (2 Sam. 9). (At that time, David also got
into trouble by stealing another man's wife . . . but that's another
story! You can find it in 2 Samuel 11.)

Oh, yes. David's other friends were real too. When David's own
son led a revolution and tried to rip the throne from David, Hushai

("Hank") stood by David in the midst of all the panic (2 Sam. 15:32–37; 17:15–16). Barzillai ("Barry"), Shobi ("Shawn"), and Makir ("Mac") remained loyal also, bringing him camping equipment and food for the family (2 Sam. 17:27–29). When everything went against him, friends like these made a difference.

And God . . . was God.

Were They Gay?

The story, right there in your Bible, is an exciting account of a tremendous friendship between two young men. One element of my tale, however, still needs clarification.

Remember the rumors about whether these two young men were gay? Jason said, "Some people are saying, well, that we are, well . . . more than friends." Those rumors were real, too, but they didn't start circulating until hundreds of years after David and Jonathan were dead.

While David and Jonathan were alive, no one questioned that they were just friends. The men hugged and, on one occasion, kissed on the cheek as they parted (1 Sam. 20:41). There was nothing sexual about this act. In those days, *all* men kissed other men when they greeted one another or parted from a friend. It was the normal, correct thing to do in that culture. It was appropriate. It was expected. If David had kissed Jonathan and no one else, some might question whether the two men were gay, but David kissed other men too, like his son Absalom and his friend Barzillai (2 Sam. 14:33; 19:39). If people say David kissed Jonathan because of sexual attraction, to be consistent, why don't they question his motive when he kissed these other men?

The whispers saying David and Jonathan were gay didn't start until this past century. Three thousand years passed by, and during all that time nobody hinted that this friendship might have been improper. The rumor is based not on the historical facts but on modern attitudes about male-male friendships. Today if men kiss each other, people suspect the men are gay. People who study the

Bible today sometimes try to reinterpret the behavior of David and Jonathan in the light of this current view.

The people who suggest that David and Jonathan were gay overlook a multitude of other males in the Bible who also kissed men. Jacob, for example, another godly man, kissed his father, his father-in-law, and his brother (Gen. 27:27; 29:13; 33:4). No one suggests that Jacob was gay, let alone incestuous.

Is Same-sex Intimacy Okay?

"So," you ask, "if men could kiss men in the days when the Bible was being written, does that mean it's okay for men to kiss men today?"

Some people would say that it is okay. They will tell you that because God didn't zap David with lightning for kissing Jonathan, God must think physical intimacy between men is okay.

But is that what we learn from this story of friendship? Remember, in *that* culture, *three thousand years ago*, people expected a man to kiss a friend on the cheek when they said hello or good-bye. If it's wrong to impose our culture's interpretations on events in Bible times, it's equally wrong to assume that cultural behaviors in the period of the Bible automatically remain the same in our times.

The focus here is not on sexual behavior. It's on cultural patterns for saying good-bye. Ask yourself, *In our society today, do people of the same sex routinely kiss as they greet each other?* It still happens in Middle Eastern cultures, but even there, kisses of greeting or farewell are not as common as fifty years ago. And where the custom continues, the kiss does not linger, is not usually on the lips, and is not reserved for a single individual.

Ah, but someone may point out that David said of Jonathan, "Your love for me was deep, deeper than the love of women!" (2 Sam. 1:26). Doesn't that statement suggest that David had feelings of homosexuality?

To understand this statement, you have to look back at the whole picture of David's life. When David became a national hero, women fell all over themselves to sing his praises (1 Sam. 18:6–7). Note the plural form of the noun in each case—*women,* not *woman.* The focus of David's statement is not a specific love relationship but a general observation about women.

Among the women who admired David was his future wife Michal. But when David later embarrassed her by dancing bare-chested in public, her love turned to scorn. When David became Saul's enemy, where were those who had once sung his praises? The people who had sung the loudest now mocked him (Pss. 22:6–8; 31:11–13). David learned that the love of women ebbed and flowed, but Jonathan remained loyal, a source of constant support. David's statement about Jonathan's love focused on his loyalty, not on sexuality.

Whenever David disobeyed the Lord, God confronted him, but nowhere in the Bible does God condemn David for his friendship with Jonathan. God sent a prophet to rebuke David when he stole another man's wife and murdered her husband (2 Sam. 12). God punished David when he relied on a military census instead of trusting God's power to protect him (2 Sam. 24:11–17). But God, who described same-sex sexual intimacy as shameful and unnatural, never accused David of doing something wrong with Jonathan. God viewed their relationship as a healthy friendship. God, in fact, delighted in the friendship because Jonathan encouraged David to seek God (1 Sam. 23:16).

God has not changed his mind about homosexuality. Our culture has.

The friendship between David and Jonathan has not changed over all these years; our culture has.

If you have a close friend who's the same sex as you and people spread rumors that you're both gay, the rumor may not reflect your specific behavior but the confusion in our culture.

That doesn't mean we can ignore our culture. After all, you and I have to live today, not in the times of David and Jonathan. We have to recognize the norms of modern culture by being even more careful and setting obvious physical boundaries in a same-sex friendship.

You must make clear that your same-sex friendship is not about physical attraction. There are times when, despite the best efforts at communication, people will misunderstand. But, through it all, don't give up investing in same-sex friendships. You can still find a level of commitment similar to that which existed between David and Jonathan.

It Is Worth the Risk!

Starting below are the stories of three people who pushed aside their fears and reached out to form healthy same-sex friendships. Two are the stories of people who themselves had unwanted homo-sexual desires; the third is an example of someone who extended friendship to a lesbian. All three individuals have allowed me to use their real names.

Dottie struggled for years in her relationships with other women. Unhealthy patterns of emotional dependency emerged each time she got close to another woman. Finally Dottie sensed God urging her to join a group of women studying the Bible. As a lesbian, she felt out of place. Week after week, grimly prepared to obey God, she forced herself to enter the room where the women met. She listened, rarely adding her own thoughts as she observed how the women related to each other.

"I gradually began going for coffee afterward with some of the women, and God used just the ordinary things of those times to show me I could have friends without all the emotional baggage I had in the past. He began to fill my same-sex love deficit through several women rather than just one."

From that larger group of women emerged a smaller group of six women, including Dottie, who continued to meet regularly. For the first time, Dottie felt part of a group, though she was the only single woman; the others were married. What began as a study of the Bible evolved into doing other activities together. The women prayed for each other. Trust relationships formed, and at last Dottie spoke openly about her struggle with lesbianism. Would they reject her?

To her utter amazement, the women continued to care for her.

Looking back years later, Dottie says, "I still get together with two or three of these friends and have no hesitation sharing any problems I have with them. One of these friends has included me as part of her extended family. I've learned about family dynamics and healthy relationships. I'm included in holiday celebrations and truly believe God sovereignly arranged this for my healing process."

Prayer Helps!

Richard discovered God could provide the friends he, too, needed. While at college, he met a professor who "was the first one who offered me hope that homosexuality wasn't the end-all sin that would send me to hell." He also met Carl, the leader of a campus club for Christians. "Fear of rejection was there every moment I thought about talking to Carl about my struggle with homosexuality. Eventually, I couldn't stay silent anymore. The years have erased the memories of his exact words, but I can still feel the warm embrace from the man I admired so much."

Graduating from college can be a difficult transition for anyone but it was especially hard for Richard to leave two trusted friends behind. In his new location, he cried out to God for help. "Lord," he prayed, "all my friends are gone . . . I have no one to talk to about my struggles! Please send a friend."

The Lord introduced him to Justin, a spiritually mature man who led a class at Richard's church. Still, Richard was not certain he should tell this man.

"Lord," he prayed a second time, "could you please give me a little something to help me know Justin is the right person to confide in?"

That week, as the two men met together apart from the class for the first time, Justin explained to Richard how one time he'd almost had sex with a man "just to see what it was like." "Pretty crazy, huh?" Justin concluded.

Not crazy at all, Richard thought! That openness was exactly what he needed to hear so he could trust Justin with his own story. "In Justin, I found a man who loved me and challenged me to grow—specifically in the area of forgiving my dad for not being everything I expected him to be. From Justin I learned that it's okay to forgive my father for not living up to my impossibly high standards. In fact, I learned that only when I released my dad from all my expectations, then and only then could I begin to receive the love God could offer. I praise God for giving me such a good friend who would be there for me and not refuse to have anything to do with me because of the nature of my struggle."

You Can Be the One God Uses!

Becky never experienced same-sex desires but she became the friend that Teri, hurting because of a lesbian past, needed.

The girls met at a weekly ex-gay support group. Becky attended because her husband was walking away from homosexuality. Teri participated because she was looking for a way out of lesbianism and trying to decide if Christ was worth living for.

Becky says, "God really has a sense of humor. Teri hated school when she was growing up and was often sent to the principal's office. What was my profession? A Christian school principal! And me? I panicked getting on and off busy freeways. What was Teri's occupation? A driver's license examiner!"

"I was a little intimidated by Teri's tough facade," Becky remembers. "It took time to gain each other's trust."

Teri knew very little about the Bible and eventually asked Becky to teach her. Teri needed accountability and encouragement to keep making wise choices about her health, her family, and life in general.

In return, Teri helped Becky when her mother fought cancer. Together they faced the loss of Becky's mom. Teri also helped Becky become more bold in making decisions, including maneuvering in heavy traffic. Both girls were richer for their friendship.

Don't Miss Out!

You may feel you don't have what it takes to build this kind of friendship. Perhaps you're afraid of what other people might say. You don't have all the answers for the questions your friend may ask.

Jonathan didn't have all the answers either. When his father tried to kill David, Jonathan felt confused about how to advise David. Jonathan knew that he himself had the right to be next in line for the throne but also that God had chosen David as the next king. Jonathan felt torn between two people he loved. He wanted to obey his father; he wanted to be there for his friend.

What could he do? Jonathan did what you and I should do whenever we feel inadequate to handle the difficult situation of a friend: He encouraged his friend to seek wisdom from God. When problems arise, don't teach your friend to rely solely on you for answers. If your male friend is gay, don't introduce him to a girl, believing that she'll be a quick fix for all his needs. Don't assume a boyfriend will fulfill a lesbian's needs. Sexual abuse has been identified as "the single factor that most propels a girl toward a lesbian identity."[1] Never push a female who has been abused by a man toward another man as the solution to her "problem." The young girl hungers to know she still has value as a woman. No man is big enough to fulfill that craving in her life.

Instead, point your friends toward Christ. Teach them to depend on God. Too many people speak only of God's condemnation of sin. You can be the one to introduce them to Christ's love, his forgiveness, and his power to help. Then, when a friend asks you a question and you don't know what to say, your friend can turn to Someone bigger than you, to Someone who has a lot more experience than you. That Someone is God.

Maybe you've been hurt like David. Perhaps your parents have torn your life apart by getting a divorce. Maybe someone pressured you to do something you wish never had happened. Maybe you're angry and can't forgive those who hurt you.

On the other hand, maybe you're more like Jonathan's father. You've hurt someone else. You've done things you're not proud of. Maybe you feel, "I dug this pit, and now it's up to me to get out of it."

Let me be honest with you. You'll never be able to climb out of that hole by yourself. You'll never be able to sew the pieces of your heart back together on your own, no matter how hard you try.

Listen to a better way. This is what God offers:

> But now God has shown us a different way of being made right in his sight—not by obeying the law but by the way promised in the Scriptures long ago. We are made right in God's sight when we trust in Jesus Christ to take away our sins. And we all can be saved in this same way, no matter who we are or what we have done. . . .
>
> God in his gracious kindness declares us not guilty. He has done this through Christ Jesus, who has freed us by taking away our sins. For God sent Jesus to take the punishment for our sins and to satisfy God's anger against us. We are made right with God when we believe that Jesus shed his blood, sacrificing his life for us. (Rom. 3:21–22, 24–25)

If you choose this better way, life still won't be easy. It takes guts to be a friend and let rumors fly around you. But you won't regret your choice. God will supply every need you have along the way.

Human friendships are always a gift from God, but never forget that your best friend is God himself.

Chew on It

1. What difference does it make that "Jason" and "Nathan" lived over three thousand years ago?

2. In the Bible, men greeted each other with a kiss. How do friends greet each other nowadays when they meet on the street?

3. When people talk about "fair-weather friends," they refer to those who only stick around when things are going okay. How could you show a friend that you are loyal? How could you teach your friends to depend on God first while still demonstrating you care about them?

4. How do you think Dottie and Richard and Teri felt before they told their friends about their same-sex desires? How did they feel when their friends accepted them?

5. What was God like three thousand years ago? Has he changed? How do the following verses answer this question?

    Whatever is good and perfect comes to us from God above, who created all heaven's lights. Unlike them, he never changes or casts shifting shadows. In his goodness he chose to make us his own children by giving us his true word. And we, out of all creation, became his choice possession. (James 1:17–18)

    Jesus Christ is the same yesterday, today, and forever. (Heb. 13:8)

Notes

Chapter 1: Help! My Friend Is Gay!

1. Bob Davies and Lori Rentzel, *Coming Out of Homosexuality: New Freedom for Men and Women* (Downers Grove, IL: InterVarsity Press, 1992).
2. Ron Belgau, "The Father Always Loves His Children," www.bridges-across.org/ba/youth/allchildren.htm.

Chapter 2: What Do I Say . . . When Friends Tell Me They Are Gay?

1. This story is found in the Bible in the book of Job. See Job 1:13–19; 2:11–13; 5:19–25; 19:13–19 for details.

Chapter 6: What Do I Say . . . When Courts Affirm Gay Marriage Is Okay?

1. Some Bible translations call this book the Song of Solomon.

Chapter 9: What Do I Say . . . When My Friend Needs Hope?

1. Bob Davies and Lori Rentzel, *Coming Out of Homosexuality: New Freedom for Men and Women* (Downers Grove, IL: InterVarsity Press, 1992).